27.45

27.45   2593
Jeffery J. Knowles
What Of The Night?

DEPRESSION

An oracle concerning Dumah:
Someone calls to me from Seir,
"Watchman, what is left of the night?
Watchman, what is left of the night?"

Isaiah 21:11

WHAT of the NIGHT

a journey through depression and anxiety

JEFFREY J. KNOWLES

Foreword by LeRoy Lawson

x

HERALD PRESS
Scottdale, Pennsylvania
Waterloo, Ontario

Library of Congress Cataloging-in-Publication Data
Knowles, Jeffrey J. (Jeffrey Jae), 1948-
    What of the night? : a journey through depression and anxiety / by
Jeffrey J. Knowles.
      p. cm.
    Includes bibliographical references.
    ISBN 0-8361-3617-9 (acid-free)
    1. Knowles, Jeffrey J. (Jeffrey Jae), 1948- . 2. Christian
biography—United States. 3. Depressed persons—United States—
Biography. 4. Anxiety—Patients—United States—Biography.
5. Depression—Religious aspects—Christianity. 6. Anxiety—
Religious aspects—Christianity. I. Title.
BR1725.K56A3 1993
248.8'6—dc20   92-37499
                                            CIP

The paper used in this publication is recycled and meets the minimum
requirements of American National Standard for Information
Sciences—Permanence of Paper for Printed Library Materials, ANSI
Z39.48-1984.

Scripture quotations are from the *Holy Bible: New International Version.*
Copyright © 1973, 1978, 1984 International Bible Society. Used by permission of Zondervan Bible Publishers.

Grateful acknowledgment is made to Harper Collins Publishers
Limited for permission to quote from *The Screwtape Letters* and *The
Voyage of the Dawn Treader,* by C. S. Lewis.

WHAT OF THE NIGHT?
Copyright © 1993 by Herald Press, Scottdale, Pa. 15683
    Published simultaneously in Canada by Herald Press,
    Waterloo, Ont. N2L 6H7. All rights reserved
Library of Congress Catalog Number: 92-37499
International Standard Book Number: 0-8361-3617-9
Printed in the United States of America
Cover and book design by Gwen M. Stamm

02 01 00 99 98 97 96 95 94 93 10 9 8 7 6 5 4 3 2 1

To Lezlee,

who stood the watch with me—
and often for me

Contents

Foreword

MILLIONS OF North Americans are depression victims. They travel incognito—only half recognized by nonpsychiatric physicians, who too often search only for some stuttering organ or system or, even wider of the mark, find "it's all in your head."

Professors and pastors offer no better diagnoses, apparently. At least this one doesn't, if his insight into the author is an indication. If ever a student of mine seemed unlikely to experience depression, he was Jeff Knowles, socially astute, emotionally cool, mentally gifted. When he enticed beautiful Lezlee Icke to marry him, who could have doubted he would one day be rich, famous, and leave a large endowment to his *alma mater*? Whether he would write the Great American Novel remained to be seen, but I knew one day his books would grace library shelves. I just never suspected he would write this one.

Depression is indiscriminate in its targets and various in its expressions. All depressions are not created equal. No age, gender, racial, religious, or social group is immune. Who expected to find in the indomitable Florence Nightingale's diary for her thirty-first year, "I see nothing desirable but death"? What companions of Lord Byron's dashing youth anticipated that he would drearily speak of his days as being in "the yellow leaf"? And though euphoria sometimes flowed from the early William Wordsworth, the older and deeper later poet lamented that he had "yielded up moral questions in despair."

Despair was a subject the collegiate Jeff Knowles knew little of. Then something—whether mid-life crisis, chemical imbalance, or life's unfathomable irreconcilables—ambushed him. Now the mature Knowles speaks with the authority that comes from having groped in the night. His is the expertise of the seasoned traveler, the initiate in the mysteries, the pilgrim who will not turn back. His is also the example of the believer who clings to the promise that "in all things God works for the good of those who love him."

Knowles' faith gives his story a happier ending than that of many victims. For example, erstwhile *New Yorker* cartoonist Ralph Barton reportedly committed suicide. He left behind a confession admitting a life of few real difficulties and an abundance of affection, attention, appreciation, and glamour. Yet he ran from wife to wife, house to house, and country to country to escape neither wife nor house nor country but only himself. He took his life, he said, because he was fed up with inventing devices for getting through the twenty-four daily hours.

Then there was Abraham Lincoln, often nearly paralyzed by despondency. One of history's touching artifacts—a yellowed newspaper clipping—was found in his pockets after his assassination. The paper had been opened so many times the edges were frayed. It was a British editorial predicting history would judge the embattled Lincoln as one of the greatest U.S. presidents. How often, in the darkness of his nights, did Lincoln reread those words, seeking to bolster slipping self-confidence?

Barton turned to suicide, Lincoln to an editorial. As you will learn, Knowles also sought and found balm for his psychic wounds. He pays tribute to medical science, to the care of a wise wife, to the power and comfort of prayer and, like Jesus in his own wilderness nights, to the sustenance of "every word that comes from the mouth of God." In addition, he shows he is more than he could have been without his uninvited tutor.

Knowles' story has particular poignancy for our family, since three of the five of us have struggled with various forms of depression, that unwelcome interloper in our home. Here Jeff has found an appreciative audience. "Yes, he's right," we say. "That's exactly how it feels. It really helps to hear someone else say it, doesn't it? And to say it so eloquently!"

You will not find the following pages an easy read. You can't skip lightly through such depths. But you can, if you will, find understanding and solace here. And hope. Especially hope.

> —*LeRoy Lawson, president, Pacific Christian College,*
> *Fullerton (Calif.); and senior pastor, Central*
> *Christian Church, Mesa (Ariz.)*

Preface

WRITING BOOKS is a curious business. Many people at one time or another give the possibility a passing thought—writing seems an easy path to fame and fortune—but perhaps especially men at mid-life dream of being authors. And so, after a few years of fantasizing about it, you one day take the plunge. It is time-consuming work, but on the whole you are pleased you could create this formidable stack of paper. You nod your head in self-congratulation, mentally checking off a big item on your accomplishments list.

Later you find out just how bad the book is. Eventually it finds its way into a musty corner downstairs, next to the broken alarm clock and botched plumbing fitting.

Whatever else it is, writing is not a glorified home improvement project. Setting aside the requisite number of Saturday afternoons and lining up the right tools, even when linked with a good idea, are not enough. Somewhere there must also be a pound of flesh invested in the process, some piece of the writer forfeited (probably not voluntarily) to the thing being written about. To mix in another image, without that irritating, intrusive piece of sand, the oyster cannot produce the defensive secretion which eventually hardens into a pearl.

What of the Night? follows a half dozen other "books" I have written—but all of those sit in stacks of paper in that musty corner downstairs. Unlike those works, this one was not delivered by a daydream and written on a roll. Rather, the impetus was a nightmare from which I could not wake, and the writing was sometimes a furious, desperate form of self-defense. At times I felt I was trying to write myself out of a black hole, but without that darkness there would have been no writing, no book. It is odd how God can hitch bright goodness to something even as debilitating as depression.

The forces of depression tell you that you are alone in the night. But I now know I had my quiet cloud of witnesses surrounding me. Among the saints already passed on were people like C. S. Lewis, who has bridged his grave with numerous books providing marvelous insights into the human condition—and God's response to it. Among the living, writers like Don Baker dared to stand beside me with frank, public admissions of their own humbling bouts with depression. Others, such as Frank Minirth, Paul Meier, Don Hawkins, and Tim Hansel, crafted words about hope and joy which the darkness could not entirely resist.

Closer to home I received good and helpful medical and personal advice from Ted Herwig, family physician; Bob McCollins, Christian psychologist; and Larry Pfahler, Christian psychiatrist. All took time to see the man behind the medical problem.

My family—wife Lezlee and no-longer-childlike children Kathi, Kim, and Mark—provided more help than they knew. Because I prefer to keep quiet about pain (except when writing books about it) I don't think the kids really saw how far away I was. Yet the family presence was, at times, all I could see to hang on to. Nevertheless, thanking them seems an odd thing—like thanking my hands for helping me write, or my brain for helping me think. Because they are a part of me, my loved ones are a part of this work.

> —*Jeffrey J. Knowles*
> *Columbus, Ohio*

"You would like to know how I behave when I am experiencing pain, not writing books about it. You need not guess, for I will tell you; I am a great coward. . . . If I knew any way of escape I would crawl through sewers to find it. But what is the good of telling you about my feelings? You know them already: they are the same as yours."[1]

> —C. S. Lewis

Prologue

IT IS five in the morning. Christmas, 1989. I wake with a start, not in excited anticipation but with a bottomless sense of dread and fear. A buzzing inside my head makes no noise, but rather takes up loud space. If I did not know otherwise I might suspect that I am running a fever, the kind which turns the night into a series of fitful spells which are neither sleep nor wakefulness, leaving you poised on the rim of darkly colored nightmares. But I know it is not a fever. How deliciously welcome a fever would be right now as an explanation, a fever caused by a good old flu bug, or even something worse—anything except this.

I sit up quickly in bed. An unfastened sense of urgency tells me to move but I don't know where or why. I grope through the darkened house and into the bathroom where I quietly take out the Xanax from my shaving kit. I sigh in misery, knowing this means another defeated day, a day lost even before the sun comes up. No matter what else happens today I will not escape the awful knowledge that I had to start it with a tranquilizer, a crutch, an open admission to myself that I am losing this war.

It's Christmas. Mom and Dad are sleeping peacefully upstairs, as are the kids and Lezlee. In a couple of hours they will sleepily open their eyes to the warm realization that the best day of the year is here. They will sense that momentary wonder, which lingers from earliest childhood, that Christmas could have come so quietly in the night. Then they will be up and embracing the special traditions of this unique day. My only goal is to survive the day, to seem chipper enough to avoid suspicion, to rearrange enough food on my plate to give the appearance of eating. I feebly pray that I can once more pull off the charade.

They say death takes no holidays. Neither does depression. It looks forward to celebrating the special torments it can produce when you are supposed to be happy. It can only do so much on a rainy day in February, when the cold winds bite and the world drowns under a sea of eternal browns and grays, and even normal people are supposed to be depressed. But on Christmas day, with colors and songs and laughter all bumping into each other in a dizzy parade of happy revelry, the opportunities are almost limitless.

On Christmas day, 1989, I was nearly five months into an emotional upheaval which was shaking me to the foundations of my existence as a human being. I was terribly fatigued, discouraged, and frightened. How long could I keep going? I wondered.

$$\mathbb{C}$$

By what road did I come to this terrible condition? The death of a child? The loss of a job? A chronic, debilitating illness? No, none of these. I could not even claim some of the blue chip causes of adult-onset depression—alcoholic parents, an abused childhood, a runaway father. There had been no teenage rage or rebellion, and no lack of loving people in my life. As Dad would say, a couple of months later when I told him the identity of my stalker, "Depression? That surprises me. You've got so much going for you."

Indeed! That was one reason this depression was so depressing. There seemed no reason for it. My job as research chief for the Ohio Governor's Office of Criminal Justice Services in Columbus is a fine one. It pays well, provides high visibility and recognition, allows me tremendous discretionary authority and flexibility, and does all of this while seldom demanding more than forty hours a week.

My marriage is enviable. In 1969 Lezlee and I joined two solid Christian families in a union which has not only survived but thrived. Lezlee is beautiful, intelligent, articulate, a superb mother, and esteemed as a successful grade school principal and assistant administrator of a thriving Christian school system. Her devotion to me is exceeded only by her tireless pursuit of her Lord. Nor do the kids offer me much of an excuse. I might have lovingly created them out of this word-processor, to my precise specifications.

At church I have been involved in every aspect of major leadership during the past decade and a half, as well as an enormously fulfilling role in that body's well-loved music ministry. My health is excellent, my friends many, my past richly endowed, my future bright with possibilities.

A therapist will often gently probe a patient's formative years to determine links to later depressions. Mine seemed to come up empty. Oh, Mom and Dad both came from homes which foundered in seas of poverty, fear, and death. Dad's mother died when he was four, and it would have been better for Mom and all of her four siblings had her father followed suit. The parts of my parents which escaped into adult lives were thrown into the world's bloodiest war in 1942. They secretly acknowledged their coming separation by eloping when they were eighteen, then spent the remainder of the war fearful that Grandpa Knowles might have the marriage annulled.

Yet somehow my parents managed to stem the floodwaters of familial failure and build a solid home for my older brother Lloyd and me. If my parents' earlier pain somehow wounded me, I at least was unaware of it. Lloyd and I grew up happily near the western wall of the cup cut by the Cuyahoga River in northern Ohio, playing baseball, picking berries, and roaming the rugged, ravined beauty of that still unspoiled region. There was a good dog, and a good school, and a good sense of family. As Dad said, I had everything going for me.

And yet. . . .

☾

Sunday, February 4, 1990: rock bottom. Sundays were generally the toughest days anyway, possibly because they are so closely associated with family and friends, probably because they were such loud reminders of the impotence of my faith. Some of my most painful and (seemingly) spiritually bankrupt moments were spent in church during the long summer/fall/winter of my discontent in 1989-90. Some of the toughest steps I have ever taken were those which started me out the back door and over to church.

Three days earlier, on Thursday, I had gone to my doctor to talk about my medication. Although I was not feeling much different, I was impressed that I had reduced my daily Xanax dosage to next to nothing—about one half of one half-milligram tablet a day. I also had it in the back of my mind to ask him about an antidepressant, something he had mentioned in the long ago days of August, 1989, when I had first gathered my fractured feelings and brought them to him.

I guess I was expecting him to be impressed with my "progress." He would either good-naturedly acquiesce to my queries about the antidepressant (I wanted him to say something like, "Well, sure, it can't hurt anything,") or gently chide me that I was doing so well I didn't need anything else.

He did neither. He was disturbed to find I was taking any Xanax at all. He reminded me of the habit-forming potential of the drug, then suggested we try an antidepressant. Lest there be anything left of my thin hopes and expectations, he made several pointed comments about how anxiety-ridden I seemed, especially in my repeated tendency to sigh deeply before speaking.

What little control I thought I had over my struggle with depression and anxiety was blown away during those few minutes in his office. The remainder of the threadbare suit was now rapidly unraveling. The last of what I thought of as hope was gone. By Sunday morning I was awash in the backwaters of despair. My seven-month ordeal was going to last a lifetime. I was sure of it. What I was not sure of was how long such a lifetime could last.

Within the nightmare I had long since lost all sense of perspective and proportion. I had pretty much given up hope that it would ever really end, and I was beginning to doubt that it had ever formally begun. The anxiety attack which had pitched me over the edge in the distant, steaming heat of a July day in a Texas hotel room now seemed vague and unimportant. I politely hosted the absurd feeling that just as this thing would go on forever, it had gone on forever. Nor were there manic peaks to compensate for life in the valley bottoms. There were no lights for the upper floors on the emotional elevator I was riding; the elevator only went down. There were, of course, some times— those endless days or interminable weekends—which were worse than others, but there were no bright patches in between, only dark grays.

℃

On Monday, August 27, 1990, I looked the devil in the eye, and he blinked. The day I had been dreading for several years, the one day which had nailed so much of my long ordeal to a one square-inch block on the calendar, had at last come to do its worst. The night before, we had said good-bye to our firstborn, Kathi, and left her on the campus of Milligan College, some 450 miles away from our home in Columbus.

I now know that more than any other single event this one had precipitated my headlong tumble into the nightmarish fun-house of emotional distortions. Like a ticking clock inside my head, this day had hounded me about the relationships I would have to give up to the past, the realities of mid-life I would have to concede to the present, and the uncertainties I would have to accept as part of a frightening future. Now that day was here.

Its pain did not disappoint me. The ordeal hurt every bit as much as I thought it would, but the part I had feared most—the part which had me convinced this whole process of Kathi's leaving home would do more emotional harm than good—failed to appear.

I no longer have to fear the way I will feel about Kathi going away, not only because it has already happened, but because I no longer have to fear pain. I am finding, more often than not, that pain is a friend—or at least a useful companion.

℃

This book is my attempt to understand a remarkable turn of events in an otherwise unremarkable life. Viewed from one an-gle, I suppose it is nothing more than another guy trying to drag a little too much ego and cowardice through the abyss we jocu-larly refer to as mid-life crisis. From another view, it may seem to be just one more human ant struggling mightily with the over-sized twigs of depression and anxiety. Millions of people have to fight those battles every day, and most manage to do so without burdening the world with a book about it.

Nor is this a story of spiritual heroism. I wish I could say that my faith never waned, that I never lost confidence in God's power and love. But that would not be true. The only living presence in whom I consistently found strength and hope throughout the entire ordeal was my wife, Lezlee.

I would, however, dare suggest that, in some ways, this account is different from others I have seen. Most notably, it is written not from the safe distance of several years, after the beast has been killed and its head mounted proudly on the wall, but from within the throes of the very battles it seeks to describe. I believe this is an important distinction. One of my main motives for translating this experience to the written page is the belief that most of the literature on depression and anxiety does not adequately *describe the feelings*. I hungered for such a resource many times in my desperate search for reassurance. Since feelings are the crux of this issue, this seemed to me an important omission.

I think I understand how this can happen. Most people in the midst of emotional torture—even writers—do not want to magnify the agony by giving it a separate life on paper. Depression and anxiety are foes we seek to avoid or, if the worst has already happened, escape. We desire no written reminders of our antagonists' presence, nor would we chance awakening them when they have seemingly dozed off.

Also, it is easy to forget the desperately painful feelings once long-term answers have been found. Quiet advice about medications, the therapeutic value of communication, and the use of spiritual principles, may make little emotional sense to those in the midst of the struggle. The thing inside of us is so huge and dominating we feel the necessity for something huge and dominating to fight it. Failing that, we at least want to be assured that our struggle is not unique, that others have suffered so and lived to benefit from it. This is why I have, throughout the work, frequently used the editorially awkward second-person, "you," in describing some of these feelings.

The importance of understanding feelings which seem, at

times, wholly incomprehensible, made me decide to be as honest as I could regarding my feelings during my emotional crisis. This decision necessarily put me close to the actual fire. I had to write while the wounds were still bleeding.

Such honesty has several costs. The first is perspective. Some of my early insights into my struggles, written during times when I was so distraught I didn't think I could physically produce one more written word on the subject, were based on misdiagnoses of my problem. The most common of these was the assumption that the real issue was anxiety when, in fact, depression was subtly and powerfully playing its hand. Two earlier episodes of emotional difficulty in my life, one coming my junior year in college six months before my marriage, the second in 1974 in Atlanta before the birth of our second child, had convinced me anxiety was the culprit.

That wrong conclusion was largely drawn from two circumstances. One was the occurrence of a major anxiety attack at the beginning of each of the multi-month episodes. The second was the specter of my mother's "nervous breakdown" in 1948 and my subsequent, lifelong assumption that I had inherited her "nerves."

Looking back, I now see that each of those two earlier struggles occurred at major change points in my life. Each was a warning tremor of the seismic emotional quake which was to rock me at mid-life. In such instances depression was driving its hellhound, anxiety, before it so effectively that I never saw anything other than the hound. At the time I would not have trifled over such distinctions. My raging anxiety, like an alcoholic's booze, seemed a worse effect than any conceivable cause.

The confusion is even present in much of the medical literature. Works on anxiety often use many of the same terms as do works on depression.[2] And the most reliable of antidepressants, Imipramine, has recently been found to be similarly effective as an anti-anxiety agent.

Doctors Raymond DePaulo and Keith Russell Ablow quote a depression patient as saying that "my days were one long, confused haze, and I was choking with fear and anxiety." Later, the doctors conclude that "severe forms of anxiety . . . may occur alone or as part of a depression."[3] At any rate, it was the symptom of anxiety, whether or not acting on its own volition, which proved to be my most discomforting companion throughout emotional upheavals, and so it frequently finds its way into this work.

Another cost of writing amidst crisis came in the form of literary indebtedness. I have probably borrowed far too frequently and freely from other authors in trying to lock onto the feelings and thoughts swirling madly around inside of me. Notably abused were the works of C. S. Lewis who, were he alive today, would probably humbly complain that he is already overquoted in Christian writing. I can only reply that these passages were of greatest help to me during my most desperate hours; they were rich spiritual manna for a starving man. I can only hope, in trusting the honesty (if not accuracy) of my feelings, that Lewis's words may also be important to others caught in a similar struggle.

The third expense of this work is invoiced to my personal pride. While neither quiet nor shy, I am somewhat private. I typically use humor or silence to dodge artfully in and out of life's tense moments. Thus many who know me probably commit the common error of assuming that since I do not do my bleeding in public I must have my life "together." God must chuckle at this; were he anybody but God he would no doubt see me as a crybaby.

The point is that I would do almost anything rather than expose weakness to public scrutiny. Looking back, I shake my head at the times I kept going for no other reason than that I could not bear the prospect of others seeing me falter. How absurd that this flimsiest of props should remain in place under me when all others had been long-since kicked out.

For that reason it has been hard to bare my soul in this way, especially now that I again feel well. I cringe as I read through diction littered with words like "agony," "pain," "turmoil," "crisis," and "torture," though I know full well that such words do not overstate what I was feeling at the time. I don't mind being a wimp, so long as no one else suspects. I constantly have to stay my hand from editing out such truths.

I know all of that is a bit silly. We have a way of twisting around our ideas of strength and weakness. In the faith context—the context in which men and women were actually created—there is no need for such poorly placed shame. If David, Paul, and Jesus could readily express their emotional anguish, why should I linger at the end of the line? It is only when we artificially secularize these problems by sucking the humanness out of a deeply human issue that we introduce shame. But knowing that does not completely free me of the burden of my pride.

☾

The chapters in this book reflect the recurring themes of my life during the year preceding this writing. Again and again the ordeal would be reduced to a hugely singular idea, an extraordinary concept with an ordinary name like "pain," or "trust," or "time." Frequently, getting a proper perspective on any one of these seemed akin to swallowing a grapefruit whole, yet I knew I would not be able to put my emotional world in order until I did so. While I cannot assume that these are textbook areas of concern for all who suffer depression, neither can I escape the belief—conveyed to me by both communication and intuition—that these are frequent visitors in the homes of the emotionally distraught.

In my case, these visitors were not content with the guest-rooms I hastily prepared for them, but insisted on taking over the entire house. Therefore I have to introduce them to you, chapter by chapter, rather like members of the family.

WHAT of the NIGHT

MORNINGS
You are not alone...

The cruelest blow comes in the morning, before you can prepare for it, before you realize what is happening. The thing is up long before you, leaning over your bed, watching intently for the first signs of your waking. Sometimes it cheats on the rules of this already unfair game; it invades those last few moments of what passes for sleep these days, sending a late nightmare to slip its icy fingers into your stomach.

When you open your eyes, you see it. There is that infinitely thin moment of nonrecognition—almost outside of time, like the clicking millisecond sandwiched between a nearby lightening bolt and its pursuing crack of thunder—then it swarms in on you.

Psychologists call it severe or extreme anxiety; it is more universally recognized as naked fear. Its most ugly, sinister characteristic is that there seems no discernable reason for it, no speech to give, no disciplinary conference with the boss, no medical report due back. It is just there, boiling at you like the bees of an invaded nest.

The prospect of the day before you stretches out like an unprepared-for journey into an endless desert. No oases are in sight. Already you feel fatigued and beaten. Last night you at least had the slim comfort of a completed day and the prospect of escape through sleep, even if sleep required a tranquilizer or sleeping pill. Now, you are suddenly back in the fray without any chance of preparing for it. You need time—even ten minutes, ten peaceful minutes—with which to arm yourself, but the thing presses right up against your face.

You do the one sensible thing you can think of. You take another tranquilizer. That seems right. Your family doctor, psychologist, and psychiatrist have all agreed such medication is necessary to block some of the negative toll anxiety is taking on your body and brain. Yes, it is the right thing to do. Yet deep inside you wonder how you are going to fare on a day that you greeted bleeding and on crutches. You yearn desperately for a few moments borrowed from one of the countless other mornings when your only concern was rain on the morning paper or a rush-hour traffic report.

How can you even begin this day with the full weight of your agitated world crushing down on you before your sleep is ended?

1

Mornings: Rudest of Awakenings

Did you tackle the trouble that came your way
With a resolute heart and cheerful?
Or hide your face from the light of day
With a craven soul and fearful?[4]

Edmund Vance Cooke

"WEEPING may remain for a night, but rejoicing comes in the morning." (Ps.30:5) What if joy doesn't come in the morning? What if first light brings not an end to, but a beginning of, the pain? Weeping at night at least provides the slim comfort that weeping is *supposed* to be done at night, that you are being somewhat orderly and sensible about your wretchedness. But what comfort is there for despair in the morning? It is not even biblical.

The anxiety of a serious depression episode is, as much as anything else, a crisis of self-confidence. It shakes every apple on the tree; nothing is invulnerable to its brutal assaults. It stands behind every heretofore stable and secure part of your life—the sleep which always came so easily and brought such freshness in the morning, the simple daily tasks done so effortlessly for years,[5] the worship service or prayer time which has so consistently refreshed your spirit—and coolly taunts, "I can get at you here, too."

27

In many ways mornings are the ultimate sanctuaries in our lives. Like miniature resurrections, they bring new hope and strength, setting us on magic carpets which bear us away from the fears and failures of yesterday and safely through the dark hours of night, where ordinary shapes and voices become twisted and loud.

As a little boy I would occasionally visit my grandmother for a summer day or two in Euclid, on Cleveland's east side. I slept on one of those glider sofas out on her screened-in back porch, my only companion a hulking streetlight glaring down at me. The worst moment of the visit came at night, when the faint squeaks of the sofa echoed the anxious noises within me—as I thought about faraway home and cowered under the menacing stare of the streetlight.

Then suddenly I was bathed in the warmth of bright sunshine. Overhead the streetlight had become a harmless dot against the blue sky. The smells of breakfast drifted out to me, and Grandma was peeking her head out of the door every two minutes to see if I had awakened. It was morning. Everything was well.

What kind of terrifying cruelty has the power to steal our mornings away? To make them emotional nighttimes with no prospect of escape? What is left when they are gone?

☾

Hannah Hurnard's well-loved work, *Hinds' Feet on High Places*, is, above all else, a story of human fear. Using the surprisingly successful and ancient technique of allegory, Hurnard's heroine, Much Afraid, stumbles from one painful failure to another. She shrinks from every circumstance, yet somehow manages to complete her fantastically difficult journey to the mountaintops. There she exchanges her crippled legs for the hinds' feet which allow her to bound across (spiritual) mountains with ease.

How did this little coward come to complete this quest? She found two oddly coupled allies, the first recognizable to Christians—desire to obey her lord (the Shepherd, in the story).

The second ally, curiously relevant to all who suffer from fears, is the realization that the undefined thing you fear—this fear of fear which we call anxiety—has overplayed its hand in crushing its victims so completely. A dog being beaten to death by its master might as well take a piece out of the offending hand since the result cannot, in any event, be any worse. Little Much Afraid, beaten into the ground by her fears, reached that ulti- mate point of weakness which, by virtue of its very helplessness and hopelessness, becomes the beginning of strength. Her sim- ple mind concluded that her only alternatives to lethal doses of anxiety were death and the Shepherd—either preferable to anxiety.[6]

Depression-born anxiety, because it is a force which seems to know no boundaries, because it invades morning and evening, church and home, workplace and hospital, becomes in time its own worst enemy. So long as we pin our hopes for beating it on some aspect of this physical world, whether counseling, exer- cise, a hot bath, or a pill, the enemy will have a target to strike. In- deed, the mere mental creation of such "safety zones" begins the process of making them vulnerable. "What if it happens here?" that little voice stage whispers before you can slap a hand over its noisome mouth. Then without a moment's respite comes the next attack: "If it happens *here* it can happen anywhere." And so the downward spiral begins again.

And yet, there is an odd if only momentary sense of relief when the parasite has finally eaten its way into the last of your treasures, when there is no more hope for physical sanctuaries. The bloated beast, having eaten itself out of a food supply, looks at you stupidly, but you can only shrug and show with a weak sweep of your hand that there is nothing left for him. Some- where in the back of your mind another sliver of comfort attach- es itself to the thought that the seemingly endless supply of ma- terial for your waking nightmares must now be exhausted.

"What more can this thing do to me than it has already done?" you ask half aloud. Suddenly the long weeks and months of anguish, which you had assumed were slowly bankrupting you emotionally, now take on the appearance of a down pay- ment on a new beginning. All that you have lost, all of your old vulnerabilities which you saw so consistently exploited, have been turned to your advantage. Now you see they have taught you the lesson that there may be more to you than these things, a part forever beyond physical limitations.

This is not the wishful thinking of someone desperately seeking a silver lining, nor merely a cute trick. Professional counselors make this same sort of suggestion to anxiety sufferers. "Try to imagine the worst thing that can happen to you," they say, "then ask yourself, 'Would that be so horrible?' " Usually for the anxiety sufferer, the worst thing imaginable is the vaguely defined idea of "losing control."

But what would losing control *actually* mean? Uncontrollable tears? A trip to the hospital? A nervous breakdown? (Psychiatrists Frank Minirth and Paul Meier state that in all their years of treating some of America's toughest anxiety cases they have never seen anyone's nerves "break down.'") Would any imagined catastrophes be irredeemable?

Not likely. People lose control of pieces of their lives all the time—to anger, passion, or to such far more dangerous masters as alcohol and drugs. Furthermore, I believe that every human being is irrationally afraid of something. The special problem during depression is that this something cannot be neatly corked in a bottle; that is why the feeling of losing control is so much stronger and more intimidating.

For others, the worst thing imaginable is death (a common fear during anxiety attacks). However, any doctor can offer the reassurance that anxiety attacks are seldom life-threatening, and that anxiety is fixable. Beyond that, doctors can remind patients that they did not invent the fear of death; it is a burden borne by all.

Simply put, when there is nothing left to lose to fear, there is nothing we need fear to lose.

Perhaps C. S. Lewis put the case best in his insightful *Screwtape Letters*. The novel is made up of a series of letters between Uncle Screwtape, a well-established bureaucrat in Satan's Lower Kingdom, and his impulsive, young nephew, Wormwood, a junior tempter forever bungling his attempts to win his human subject to the Prince of Darkness. Screwtape wisely admonishes his nephew to remember that humans are winnable to Satan only as long as they retain false hopes. Once they despair of all of their artificial props in life they are not, as the incompetent Wormwood would happily believe, closer to Satan, but rather to God.

> It is after men have given in to the irremediable, after they have despaired of relief and ceased to think even a half hour ahead, that the dangers of humbled and gentle weariness begin. . . . Whatever he *says*, let his inner resolution be not to bear whatever comes to him, but to bear it "for a reasonable period"—and let the reasonable period be shorter than the trial is likely to last. It need not be *much* shorter; in attacks on patience, chastity, and fortitude, the fun is to make the man yield just when (had he but known it) relief was almost in sight.[8]

In another passage Screwtape hits even closer to the mark of the anxiety sufferer. He vigorously warns his easily distracted nephew,

> Do not be deceived, Wormwood. Our cause is never more in danger than when a human, no longer desiring but still intending to do our Enemy's will, looks round upon a universe from which every trace of him seems to have vanished, and asks why he has been forsaken, *and still obeys.*[9] (emphasis added)

What remarkable comfort is contained in that thought. For if true, it means that what may be the very moment of deepest agony—perhaps in the early sunlight of a day which seems to stretch out endlessly before you—actually dwells the beginning of strength. It means that the wounds you feel are not the work of a mindless slasher who would take your life but of a skilled surgeon who would give it to you, and give it more abundantly. Somewhere this side of masochism there is room to be comforted, not in spite of, but because of the pain you are feeling.

MEDICATIONS
You are not alone...

You feel like the Ray Milland alcoholic character in "Lost Weekend," stashing bottles in secret and strategic locations around the house. But in this case the bottles contain not booze but pills—Valium or Xanax, perhaps—something which will rudely broadcast to the world that you, like Ray, aren't quite strong enough to make it through the day on your own. And though your spouse knows about and understands your need for medication, you find yourself taking your daily doses in secret.

Nights are worse. When you have battled the night terrors as long as you dare, you ease out of bed with the stealth of a burglar and tiptoe comically to the bathroom, silently cursing each creak of the flooring. When you open the cupboard a poorly placed jar of something thuds to the floor. She stirs in the bed. You pour out the tablets with infinite care, but in the huge stillness they sound like a baby's rattle. She calls out to you, and you cringe, caught in the middle of a shameful felony.

Even the bright sunshine can expose the many tripwires of the medication hassle. The blood drive at work to which you have always cheerfully donated. A request that you drive some children on a long trip. The list of ingredients on the back of the cold medicine which had always worked so well for you. The blood workup on your preemployment physical. The slim supply of clever comments to cover your sudden sweats, cold hands, or momentary dizziness. When time permits, you entertain the Dalai Lama of all worries, the thought that while you cannot live without your medication, neither can you live with it.

But worst of all is the perpetual sense of weakness which accompanies the specter of psychotropic (mood-altering) drugs. Using them shames you, no matter how persuasive the arguments of your doctor that they fill the same roles as aspirin, erythromycin, or prednisone. The faint voice of reason further argues the infantile absurdity of a nation in which a "hard-drinking man" is viewed as admirably tough while his prescription-taking counterpart is assumed to be a wimp.

But you cannot quite bring your acceptance in line with your logic. What does dependency on a medication say about you as a man, where crutches are viewed with contempt? Or as a Christian, where hundreds of Scriptures remind you that God alone is sufficient for your needs? Or as a father, where deeds always speak louder than words?

And now you begin to wonder: Which is the real enemy? Your emotional problem? Or the medication?

2

Christians and Medications: Strangers in a Strange Land

Is there no balm in Gilead?
Is there no physician there?
Why then is there no healing
for the wound of
my people?
Jeremiah 8:22

JOE BOB BRIGGS is a nationally syndicated columnist whose gift to humanity is his capacity to explain the difference between the real and the phony in our complicated world. Lest that rare talent be lost on his simple readers, Briggs punctuates the fact with a barrage of down-home hints, like regular-guy grammar ("wanna" for want to and "em" for them) and a large cowboy hat to adorn his pictured byline.

On March 27, 1990, Joe Bob came riding out of the west Texas sunset to set the nation straight about Prozac, the tremendously popular antidepressant, which had just finished another successful run, this time on the cover of *Newsweek* (March 26, 1990). In an article entitled "Pop a Prozac and woes will end—or will they?" Joe Bob lassoed and hog-tied thirty-five years of research in the use of psychotropic drugs with some straight-shooting. He informed his readers that Prozac is a happy pill for wimps and weirdos, and that the best way to handle depression is to have your minister remind you not to spend so much time thinking about yourself. Briggs confidently concludes, "So, you see, a lot of what this [taking Prozac] is is taking people who are already ready for Looney Tunes—and making 'em a *little less* looney."[10]

Without jingling his spurs, Briggs proceeded to herd all of the remaining Prozac users—presumably those not quite ready for Looney Tunes—into the category of drug abusers. He referred to the high price of Prozac as if talking about a heroin score ("$1.60 per hit") and characterized the treatment for employment-related depression as a quick grab for a fix: "Lost your job? . . . Pop a Prozac! You still don't have a job, but you feel great about not having a job."[11]

The Briggs editorial is remarkable for more than its audacity. The fact that it even got printed speaks volumes about the popular mentality regarding such medications. In a day when journalists are being suspended for rumored racial slurs, Briggs's callous indictment of at least fifteen million Americans guilty of nothing more than illness seems to beg a severe response. We can only imagine the thunderous cry for his scalp had Briggs directed his sniggering misinformation at AIDS patients. Yet two months after the publication of his column, Joe Bob Briggs was still unmolested in his casual pursuit of journalistic excellence. Neither did the *Columbus Dispatch* feel the need to print any retraction or apology.

But, in fairness to Briggs, his sentiments concerning both emotional problems and drugs used to treat them are probably not far off the beaten path of American public opinion. Another recent editorial page offering, this one from Enid and Richard Peschel, cited a poll by the National Alliance for the Mentally Ill. The poll found that 71 percent of the public attributed mental illness to emotional weakness, 65 percent cited bad parenting, and 43 percent placed the blame on the victims themselves.[12]

Such findings are illuminating. If Americans see serious mental illness in terms of character defects, how much more severely will they judge the greater number of people who suffer the less dramatic but no less painful debilitations of serious depression and anxiety?

The fictions about emotional difficulties are probably on their way to full exposure, but there is evidence that they will die long and hard. As I was reading the Briggs article, I was reminded of a headline I had seen in a 1906 Atlanta newspaper while doing thesis research. Matter-of-factly written under the blaring headline about a flood in Oklahoma was the subhead, "No Whites Among the Dead." The social distance between 1906 and 1975 jolted me in the quiet of that library, so much so that I was worried someone passing by might glimpse my reading material. In another decade or two, someone reading Joe Bob Briggs' column may experience a similar culture shock. But not now. Not yet. And a decade or two is a long time to wait when you're in the frozen depths of depression.

This transition time in societal awareness hosts some odd public images. In 1972, just eight years before the nation would casually elect its first divorced president, George McGovern's campaign was greatly damaged by the disclosure that his running mate, Senator Thomas Eagleton, had suffered emotional problems during an earlier period in his life. Responses were interesting and telling. The Republicans smiled smugly, relieved that this genuine campaign issue would blow away the minor PR problem they were having with that embarrassing little break-in at the Watergate Hotel.

For their part, the Democrats fretted, as if caught with their hands in the cookie jar, and fumed that careless background investigations had not unearthed this damning bit of evidence. McGovern's response—or so it seemed to me—was simply to carry on bravely even though inflicted with this mortal wound, perhaps hopeful that his courage could capture votes where his judgment could not.

Around the country political observers sadly shook their heads at this abrupt end to the campaign. Everyone rightly assumed that this one fact, an ancient association with a "mental problem," would torpedo Eagleton *and* McGovern. No one stood to proclaim, as at least some would a few years later when

Gary Hart was caught in a web of infidelity, that Eagleton's former emotional problems did not compromise his present capacity to lead the nation. No one dared believe, as people had demonstrated in electing Franklin Roosevelt to four terms, that a physical problem should bar a man from the presidency—for no one dared suppose Eagleton's former problem was anything other than a character defect.

Two decades later we talk a better game, but the stigma remains. Press agents and political spokespersons rush to media microphones to grimly announce that their main man or woman is suffering from exhaustion, and that is why they haven't been seen in public for a week. The word "exhaustion" is redeemable. It carries a certain noble quality with it, like "battle fatigue." The terms "breakdown" or "emotional collapse," however, portend singular political disasters. Voters will allow you to recover from exhaustion, but not from a breakdown, even when such terms refer to the same difficulty.

((

There are two questions behind a Christian's hang-up with seeking psychiatric treatment in general, and taking mood-altering medications in particular. The first is, "What will my Christian family and friends think of me?" Inherent in that question is the amazingly durable assumption, already ancient in the days when Jesus challenged the hypocritical attitudes of the Pharisees, that faith is more form than substance. Better to quietly suffer all manner of agony than to openly admit the existence of a problem.

This twisted bit of reasoning puts the Christian on the same moral plane with the legendary boy revered by Sparta's military teachers. The boy continued to coolly lie about the stolen fox under his coat even when the half-crazed animal began tearing the flesh away from the boy's heart.

The second question, by far the better of the two, is, "What will God think of me?" Unfortunately, we are less likely to ask this question than the first. Or if we do, we simply lump God and his projected responses in with those we fear from our Christian family and friends. "My people do not need chemical crutches," we think we hear God scolding. "If your faith were strong enough you would not need tranquilizers or antidepressants. Those are the world's answers to problems. I alone am everything you will ever need."

On the surface, the question concerning the responses of Christian friends and family would seem to merit little response. It represents one of those dreary practices people are forever condemning in Sunday school classes but faithfully observing during the week's remaining 167 hours. Form over substance will always have a comfortable place in religion. Yet it is worth noting that even here, in the depths of admitted hypocrisy, God is willing to reach us on our own ground if we offer him no other. God shrugs, probably a little disgustedly, but then decides to throw us the life-preserver anyway, even though he has to throw it around the corner where we have retreated.

I believe God did this for me in my psychological battle with Xanax. As I have said, I could not use that medication without feeling guilt. Aside from failing to address my depression, which I did not understand at the time, I saw the Xanax as a constant reminder that something was "wrong" with me. Any healing would have to be measured, at least in part, by my capacity to put distance between myself and that drug.

That, in fact, is what I was allowed to do. When I began taking an almost immediately effective antidepressant, Imipramine, I experienced a double benefit, since the good impact of that medication was supplemented by a sense of achievement in weaning myself from the tranquilizer (which has a greater potential for habit-forming abuse.) To this day I do not know how much of my remarkable turnaround in February and March, 1990, was due to Imipramine, and how much to my perception that I had whipped Xanax. Even silly mental games can produce significant victories.

But back to the better question. What does God really think about such things? What would God say if, childlike, you were to appear before him and say, "Lord, I've been feeling terrible lately, so terrible that I don't know if I can keep on going. I'm so confused and tired and afraid that I can't do anything with the truth even when I hear it. Do you suppose I could take some medicine for a while to help me get back on my feet?"

To the extent that this limited mind can anticipate God's answer, I believe God would begin by reminding you that the material of this world, whether pills or plowshares, is created neither good nor bad. It acquires goodness or badness based on our use of it. This was Paul's painfully drawn conclusion, given to the Corinthian Christians squabbling over whether to eat meat originally offered as sacrifices to the pagan gods. "Food does not bring us near to God; we are no worse [spiritually] if we do not eat, and no better if we do," Paul says (1 Cor. 8:8).

The apostle's normally vehement adversary, Screwtape, agrees with him on this point. Speaking of the possible advantages to be gained for Satan when humans fall in love—and are properly manipulated—Screwtape reminds his nephew that "Like most of the other things which humans are excited about, such as health and sickness, age and youth, or war and peace, it [falling in love] is, from the point of view of the spiritual life, mainly raw material."[13]

Beyond this is the more tempting possibility—although too easily turned into rationalization for abuse—that God actually intended for us to trip upon such discoveries as tranquilizers and antidepressants. Certainly it would be difficult to draw the line on such intentions, to say that while God probably approves of artificial insulin and polio vaccines he would never extend such approval to medications for the mind. Even alcohol, the grand champion of substance abuse in the history of humankind, does not draw God's total disfavor. Aside from that embarrassing (to teetotalers) first miracle of Jesus at the wedding feast in Cana, there are other biblical references not unfriendly to wine. I remember that a good friend of mine, new to the church and anxious to see just how restricting this new commitment was going to be, once excitedly proclaimed the virtues of Proverbs 31:7-8. That text specifically orders "strong drink" for the depressed and the poor.

There are other and better reasons why I believe God would look kindly on requests for medicinal relief from emotional pain. The first reason is the doctrine of "divine refreshment" which, of course, was never allowed to become a doctrine at all since those charged with identifying our doctrines for us immediately spotted its potential for abuse. Nevertheless, God's desire to give us needed refreshment and replenishment along troubled roads is unmistakably present in the scriptural accounts of his handling of his saints. Minirth and Meier frequently use this principle in treating patients. Citing Elijah, so ravaged by anxiety in his dangerous battles with Jezebel that he was ready to succumb to depression's death wish, the doctors note

> that God's treatment didn't begin with talk or advice. First there was sleep, then food, then more sleep. Only after he [Elijah] was completely refreshed and had taken the physical steps to shake his depression did God allow Elijah to continue the forty-day trek to the mountain.

Not surprisingly, the doctors conclude that "We often prescribe total rest as the first phase of treatment for patients hospitalized for anxiety disorders."[14]

C. S. Lewis believed that God is much more likely to grant our requests for respites than those for happiness.

> We are never safe, but we have plenty of fun, and some ecstasy. It is not hard to see why. The security we crave would teach us to rest our hearts in this world and oppose an obstacle to our return to God: a few moments of happy love, a landscape, a symphony, a merry meeting with our friends, a bathe or a football match, have no such tendency. Our Father refreshes us on the journey with some pleasant inns, but will not encourage us to mistake them for home.[15]

During my ordeal God consistently allowed me two such pleasant inns along the difficult way. One came in the form of physical exercise. Not once did that activity fail at least temporarily to lift my despairing spirit (a little detail God saw to untold eons ago when his infinitely creative hand decreed that there should be such a thing as endorphins). This was a remarkable replenishment, given that the rages of anxiety and depression had often left me with flu-like symptoms by the time I got to my three-mile run at the day's end. The second consistent respite came in the form of a wonderful listener and good psychologist, Bob McCollins, a Christian counselor whose sessions convinced me that "therapy" was not a dirty word.

Sometimes God's refreshments are so pristinely good that we feel guilty about enjoying them. Something within us immediately warns, "There must be a catch to it!" or, less cynically, "Something this good can't be this easy." This tendency is illustrated in the old joke about the man who, strong and proud in his Christian faith, sat serenely on his rooftop as rising floodwaters crept up toward him. No less than three would-be rescuers came to his aid—in two boats and a helicopter—but he spurned each offer with the confident assertion that his God would save him. Soon after, the raging waters overtook him, and he died. When he reached heaven he could not resist questioning the Lord's failure to honor the man's great faith that he would be divinely saved. The Lord replied, "I sent two boats and a helicopter, what more did you expect?"

I was similarly suspicious of the dramatic turnaround in my emotional health when I made the transition from Xanax to Imipramine. I could not let myself believe that a few tablets with a combined bulk about equal to one undersized lima bean could not only end my nightmare but also let me feel better than I had in a decade. In fact, such was my sense of economy about that incredible bargain that I was actually grateful for the sometimes significant side-effects of the medication, because they helped relieve me of the obligation I felt to make at least some payment for this marvelous gift.

The third reason why I believe God does not begrudge us medical help in times of emotional crisis—once we have learned the lessons such crises maybe meant to teach—is that life is too short to be spent in unnecessarily long periods of agony. Minirth, Meier, and Hawkins identified their most severe case of anxiety as a woman who had suffered the rages of that sickness for sixteen years. Although they were able to help Linda J., the doctors sadly concluded that no one should have to suffer that kind of agony on earth. Those sixteen years were redeemable but not replaceable. Gone forever were Linda's marriage, precious years with her children, physical beauty, and the promise afforded by her remarkable talents and personality. Would God have objected had Linda stumbled on the Minirth-Meier clinic at the front-end of those sixteen years?[16]

James Dobson describes a similar tragedy in the case of his own mother. For many years, following menopause, Mrs. Dobson was tormented by severe emotional problems. Deprived of a proper supply of estrogen, as well as proper understanding of the problem, she spent what might have been good years fearfully walking on the outer edges of sanity.[17] What a terrible waste of a good human being! It is not likely God would require this kind of suffering for want of a simple body chemical. Unlike the Greek gods, our God takes no pleasure in the capricious misery of mortals.

However, medication does not absolve us of our need for accountability. Much of this chapter has focused on seeing severe emotional difficulties as physical rather than personal issues. Changes in body chemistry may so incapacitate us that only a physical solution will do. But there is danger here. Removing illegitimate guilt is not the same as removing all guilt for the disease. Frequently we are contributing authors to our wretched plays, and everyone adds at least something to the script.

Often there is a good initial excuse. Some people lose a family member or a job. I had lost a hope. As a result I had several years of lightly resisted negative emotions invested in my ordeal before it rocked me in the middle of 1989. For too long it had been too easy, too deliciously easy, to find comfort in the company of self-pity and anger—what San Diego clinical psychologist Michael Yapko referred to as anger turned inward.[18] Well, then, let the poison-bearers come! Their dark and richly fermented brew allowed me to spite the heavens.

The mental and spiritual habits which led to the darkest year of my life were largely of my own making. While I cannot be blamed for distilling anger, self-pity, and selfishness, I did imbibe heartily when the cup was passed around.

I could hardly blame someone else for the hangover.

PAIN
You are not alone . . .

You call it by the names most familiar to you—pain, fear, suffering, hurt—but these don't seem to fit what you feel. The thing inside of you maintains a life of its own and plays by its own rules.

The first rule is that nothing is beyond the reach of depression's scythe-like sweep. Pride, past, people, places, prayers—all are fair game for it. The second rule is that time no longer means what it did before. No doctor can tell you when the pain will go away, or when it may return again. There is the feeling, which becomes almost a conviction, that no amount of time will allow you ever to feel well (normal!) again.

In your head you hear Jimmy Stewart's plea to his guardian angel, Clarence, in the classic Capra film, *It's a Wonderful Life*, "I want to *live* again!" But the endless agony of the next five minutes tells you that it will never happen, that life has closed the window on contentment and opened the door to despair.

The third rule, and the worst, is that depression demands compound interest on its investment. Once it unleashes its initial fury of disorienting confusion, it demands that you keep up the game by losing your perspective on everything. Suddenly you are putting every part of your life under the microscope of "normalcy," which of course destroys any chance of normalcy. As each part of your life slides out of focus, this part in turn throws some other part out of sync. You are left, seemingly, with no place from which to make a stand.

And help seems nowhere in sight.

3

Pain: Defined, Redefined, Redeemed

*(He) Who doomed to go in company with Pain
And Fear and Bloodshed, miserable train!
Turns his necessity to glorious gain;
In face of all these doth exercise a power
Which is our human nature's highest dower;
Controls them and subdues, transmutes, bereaves
Of their bad influence and their good receives.* [19]

William Wordsworth

IT IS a fair bet that most people who suffer from depression would prefer that physical difficulties were the problem rather than the symptoms. A physical problem has a physical cause, hence a physical solution. Physical problems take their expected places in the world of time; a throbbing finger requires X hours of pain, a flu bug Y days, and recovery from surgery Z weeks.

Doctors will tell you that depression also exists in the worlds of cause and effect and time. They say that anxiety is a physical problem, triggered directly by adrenaline levels and perhaps (recent research hints) by the brain response in certain people.

I am neither qualified nor inclined to doubt these explanations; they are consistent with much of my own experience with anxiety. No matter. The point is that the pain of emotional an-

guish doesn't *feel* the same as physical pain. Perhaps one difference between the two is that while we have dealt with physical
pain since infancy we are much less experienced with mental
pain. There is little context for it in our lives.

My conscience compels me to put on the brakes long enough
to hear from the people who really know something about physical pain. I am not one. A couple of broken bones from high
school football and the usual assortment of cuts, bruises, and flu
aches is insipid stuff compared to the diet of pain digested by
Tim Hansel, whose mountain climbing fall in 1974 left him with
little unbroken in his back and searing pain dented only by
5,000-7,000 milligrams of aspirin every day. (Interestingly, when
Hansel can make it out of bed to speak or write, his subject is
joy.[20])

There are countless others who suffer through the pain of
cancer or arthritis without feeling compelled to write a book
about it. Who am I to suggest that their anguish is less than that
caused by emotional turmoil? Probably most people—certainly
most young people—would not see it that way. I vividly remember a moment in a church camp class when we were discussing
what we thought were the worst kinds of human suffering. All of
us kids described terrible physical ordeals which we had imagined or witnessed. We were baffled by the teacher's refusal to be
greatly impressed by any of these.

"What could be worse?" we asked.

This minister of many years responded, in a tone suggesting
that he thought everyone in the world already knew, "Why, a
lost soul!"

While a lost soul does not necessarily equate with emotional
distress, the type of pain probably does. It has to do with that
word "lost." R. Harvard, writing an appendix on pain for C. S.
Lewis's *The Problem of Pain*, concludes that "mental pain is less
dramatic than physical pain, but it is more common and more
hard to bear."[21] Minirth, Meier, and Hawkins state that some
people are so intimidated by an emotional problem that they
"prefer that a physical problem be the culprit, and they won't
stop until they find a doctor who agrees."[22]

A physical problem was certainly my preference the first

time I encountered severe anxiety. I can remember thinking that it would almost be a relief if a doctor told me my problem was cancer. That sounds insultingly flippant to anyone so afflicted, and I realize I would feel different if I actually had cancer. But the point is that to the outside observer, at least, it seems even cancer obeys some logical rules.

Depression-driven anxiety, on the other hand, is a renegade, exulting in the lawlessness with which it tears at you. It is hard to get a handle on something which has no handle. Small wonder depression is so readily accompanied by a feeling of lostness.

The pain of this lostness is incredibly difficult to describe; so difficult, in fact, that had I not intellectually convinced myself that millions of other people also experience it (emotionally, I cannot convince myself that anyone else experiences it!) I would never have begun this book. The words do not do justice to the feelings. When I try to explain those feelings to friends who have never felt them, a hint of puzzlement squeezes into eyes otherwise filled with genuine love and concern. I wonder if they suspect hypochondria. It makes me feel like the sweating, sickly heroes in those cheap 1950s science fiction films who, dressed in suits which never got wrinkled, were forever running about the city trying to convince the police chief/newspaper editor/army commander that the town had been invaded by giant seed pods/giant ants/giant flies.

On a higher plane, I am reminded of Remarke's (*All Quiet on the Western Front*) youthful World War One German combat veteran who, when he went home on leave, could find no one to talk to about his experiences at the front. None of them understood about combat because none had experienced it. Likewise, no one who has not felt the pain of depression can fully understand it.

C

While we differ about the severity of pain there seems little disagreement among Americans as to the value judgment to be placed on it—it is an unmitigated evil to be avoided at all costs. Lewis says that this instinctive reaction against pain was so strong in him that, in the aftermath of some terrible ordeal during which God had stayed especially close to him, he found himself deliberately avoiding God. God had become a painful reminder, by association, of that difficult time.[23]

Typically, to make some broad generalizations, Americans handle pain in two stages. The first sees them trying to get rid of it as quickly as possible. This is probably the flip side of the "instant gratification" records which play so well in our society. Failing this, most people move to the second stage, featuring the "tough it out/be a man" approach, certainly a cut above stage one but hardly deserving the high status it claims in the old John Wayne westerns.

A couple of hours in front of the TV or in a store will convince most foreign observers that Americans are virtually devoid of patience. We will not, with any particle of grace, wait for anything. Standing in a bank line or sitting in rush-hour traffic brings out in us the outrage of one whose constitutional rights have been violated.

Once a year in Columbus, never more, it snows enough to snarl traffic, close schools, and make a general mess of things. The day after, radio talk-show phone lines are jammed with irate callers who were an hour or two late getting home. They castigate city officials for failing to provide an adequate number of trucks and crews to handle the city's once-a-year event. Their reasoning, when held up to the light of simple math, means that the city should invest an additional one to three million dollars in trucks which will sit in the city garage 364 days a year so citizens can be spared one wait of less than two hours. And this demand comes from people who have had a day to think about it.

Neither do we have any patience with pain. Advertisers for relief of nasal congestion, headaches, and upset stomachs emphasize that their advantage over the competition lies not in how well but how *fast* they work—seconds instead of minutes, minutes instead of hours. The two underlying and unspoken assumptions in this kind of appeal are first, that most of us are cowards about pain; and second, that pain is an unmixed evil.

The prospect of coexistence with pain is abhorrent; the possibility that pain may contain within it some redemptive good is not even imagined. The sole idea is to be rid of it in the shortest possible time.

Our exception to this rule comes in the form of a distant admiration for people who manage to accomplish remarkable tasks while burdened by some great pain or handicap. We admire the football player who performs well despite a painful hip. We respectfully shake our heads through *Reader's Digest* articles about people who have overcome their pain. We think it amazing that they could accomplish so much *despite* their pain. It seems never to occur to us that their pain might have been the beginning of their strength.

We are also willing to admire our own bouts with pain, but only from the safe distance of several months for physical pain, and several years for mental or emotional anguish. We feel a sense of pride for having persevered, and enjoy telling others how much we suffered (suffered, yet still managed to remain the remarkable person you see standing before you today!). But this is as far as most of us dare go. Better to keep the thing locked away in the closet, hoping it will stay quiet and not realize its own prodigious strength when riled. Anything that hurts that badly must be, in fact, bad.

☾

While most of our society sees pain as an evil to be avoided, there are some who keep quietly insisting that there is more to it than that. They argue that pain, like all of life's experiences, contains within it the seeds of greater stuff.

There is a scene from an old Orson Wells movie in which he plays the patriarch of a large southern family. He is explaining to someone (Paul Newman, I think) why he won't take his pain medicine for a particularly excruciating form of cancer. "At least the pain is real—it reminds me that I am still alive," he says, or words to that effect. The suggestion is that suffering is neither the only nor perhaps the most dominant characteristic of pain. There is something more.

The Bible frequently makes the same point, sometimes bluntly (the crucifixion), sometimes subtly (Paul's "thorn"). Especially intriguing, and ultimately encouraging, is the idea that pain *leads* somewhere, that there is some purpose in it other than the arbitrary falling of nature's heavy hand.

James' well-known challenge to "consider it pure joy, my brothers, whenever you face trials" (James 1:2) does not conclude with a cheery "things are bound to get better," or "keep a stiff upper lip, old boy." Rather, it ends with the assertion that pain is part—an absolutely indispensable part—of a directional process which leads through perseverance to ultimate self-sufficiency ("mature and complete, not lacking in anything"). A suffering Paul draws the same conclusion in his letter to the Christians in Rome when he ties suffering into the threads which weave together endurance, then character, then hope—a hope which does not disappoint.

In *The Voyage of the "Dawn Treader,"* a boy named Eustace Scrubb finds that he has been turned into a dragon. By normal standards of fantasy this should prove to be no great obstacle, but even in the world of imagination this all but overwhelms poor Eustace, the consummate sissy. He has made his involuntary journey aboard the ship, *Dawn Treader,* an unending squall of complaints, threats, and tears. His cousins, already two books into C. S. Lewis' wondrous world of Narnia and joyfully anticipating another romp, are at wits end with what to do about Eustace—until he becomes a dragon.

Eustace thought himself miserable as a pampered English schoolboy (he called his parents by their first names and enjoyed looking at pictures of fat foreign children doing exercises). But now, whisked away on a Narnian sloop of war, he learned as a dragon the true meaning of wretchedness. Forced to live inside cold, scaly skin, and to subsist on a diet of other dragon meat, the boy despaired of all hope. Lest he forget his miserable state for a moment there was a constant, searing pain in his left front paw where a stolen bracelet, once greedily slipped onto the thin wrist of a boy, now cut deeply into his newfound flesh and bone.

But his greatest agony came on the day he changed back into a little boy. That transformation required a series of snakelike skin sheddings, each peeling more painful than the last. The very last shedding was done by Aslan himself, the great lion of

Narnia. Later, as a refreshingly humbled Eustace related the episode to his cousin, Edmund, he said,

> The very first tear he [Aslan] made was so deep that I thought he
> had gone right into my heart. And when he began peeling the skin
> off, it hurt worse than anything I've ever felt. The only thing that
> made me able to bear it was just the pleasure of feeling the stuff
> peel off. You know—if you've ever picked the scab of a sore place.
> It hurts like bully-oh but it is such fun to see it coming away.[24]

Nor was that the end of either Eustace's pain or pleasure. He
proceeded to tell Edmund, who had had enough dealings with
Aslan to believe every word of the story, that the lion then
roughly grabbed the pink-skinned boy and threw him into a
pool of cold water. This caused one more long moment of real
pain but was followed by a joyous swim which Eustace described as "perfectly delicious."

I thought often of Eustace and his dragon skins while agonizing through lost months of depression and anxiety. After a long
day or a series of long days, when feeling as if every ounce of my
comfortable old life had been body-slammed out of me, I
stopped to wonder if the process was destroying a healthy life or
cleansing an unhealthy one. I was struck by a sensory image of
having been scoured out on the inside with a stiff wire brush and
an abrasive cleanser. The scrubbing was brutally painful, since it
removed dirt which had, for years, insulated vulnerable feelings.
But surely anything which hurt that badly must be
bad . . . mustn't it?

One of my more helpful prayers during those months went
something like this. "Okay, Lord, for better or worse, I'm pretty
much empty now—empty, but clean. If you've got something
you've been trying to get inside of me, now would probably be a
good time."

The prayer has not been in vain. I am curiously fascinated by
the way my life has taken on qualities nowhere in evidence a
year ago. More about those later; for now, it is enough to say that
prior to the sweep of pain's wire brush, there was simply no
room for such qualities.

Major corrective surgery plays a similar role. The mental

preparation is anguishing and the recuperation often long and painful. It is frequently true that at no one moment in the patient's life did the problem necessitating the surgery *hurt* as much as the surgery itself. A hundred times, during the long days of recovery, patients may wonder what madness possessed them to trade the problem for the cure.

But it does not end there, just as Eustace's delicious swim did not end with the first painful encounter of raw skin and cold water. Postoperative pain does cease, and in its place comes the awareness that an old problem—a pain, a restriction, an embarrassment—has been forever removed. Patients, like Eustace, may then spend a good deal of time delightfully splashing around in their newfound deliverance.

Some medical people might be troubled by such analogies. Anxiety and depression are medical problems, they might argue, which have damaging consequences if untreated and frequently stem from some earlier and unmistakably bad experience, such as alcoholic, abusive, or obsessive parents. In my own difficulties I can readily identify other negative factors, few of which related directly to my growing up years, which led to emotional problems. It is medically and spiritually unsound to conclude that God creates such negative factors to bring about cleansing in our lives. I do not believe God authors such causes—or at least not nearly so many of them as we think.

However, God did create the rules of cause and effect, and therein lies our hope. No matter what truly bad conditions fathered emotional distress, or what kind of real danger lies in the failure to deal with it properly, it is likely that this seemingly lethal weapon can also be used as a spiritual tool. Minirth and Meier repeatedly state that anxiety can be friend as well as foe. Similarly, Lewis's or Harvard concludes that "if the cause [of mental pain] is accepted and faced, the conflict will strengthen and purify the character and in time the pain will usually pass."[25]

This is James 1 revisited and Romans 8:28 as well—a verse which has particularly troubled me over the years. During those awkward moments at funeral parlors, when squirming for something appropriate to say to the family of the deceased, I could never use, "All things work together for good for those that love the Lord." This was especially true if "all things" included a child killed by a drunk driver or leukemia. Neither did the words seem right for house fires, split churches, or life support systems.

But my strenuous struggle with depression has opened my eyes to the realization that the key is not "all things" which work for good. The key, rather, is God, who in all things works for good. This does not mean we always experience a net gain, especially on the heels of tragedy. It does not prevent our wanting to undo tragedy if given the opportunity. It only means that the author of cause and effect intended that his creation should always contain within it the pull of forward direction. There would be much stumbling, but there needn't be falling.

Interestingly, as is true of all of God's creation principles, this one works equally well when shorn of biblical language. The mother of a child afflicted by a rare disease desperately seeks other parents facing the same trauma. Her road is rough at first, winding through dozens of bemused hospital officials to cautious voices on the other end of telephone lines, voices which betray the fear of being hurt again.

Eventually a small, nervous group meets in her home one night. After an awkward start each mother begins to express the feelings she heretofore thought were uniquely and painfully her own. By evening's end they are basking in the therapeutic warmth of shared problems and eagerly planning more meetings. The group grows, then branches out to form other groups.

Soon there are support groups all over the city, and the original mother, who knows a family facing the disease in a neighboring state, wonders what number of people might be in similar agony nationwide.

A quantum twenty-year leap finds her the national director of an organization with thousands of members, several publications, a regular radio broadcast, and an office in Washington, D.C. Suddenly, in the midst of a typically harried day, she is struck by the question: "What would my life have been like had my child been normal"?

How many times has this scenario been acted out, albeit less dramatically, in the lives of people facing problems? It is another of God's beautiful subtleties—when the ends seem unbearable God sometimes allows us to find answers in the means.

☾

Now comes a tantalizing possibility: If pain is something more than curse to be cured or endured, if it is something which can actually make us better than we were before, is it possible pain may paradoxically be the door to life's most elusive prize—joy?

Not so long ago, I would have quickly dismissed this idea as the desperate rationalizing of those whose lives are perpetually in turmoil. It takes neither a logician nor a psychiatrist to see that pained people are unhappy people, and that talk of joy through suffering would be swept out the door if the sufferer had half a chance to unload the pain at the expense of the rationalization. Such talk once seemed nothing more than the need of struggling people to hang on to something, even a silly something, during times of intense trouble.

My certainty about all of this has now, like many other things in my life, disappeared. My only excuse for the brazen and over-simplified judgment of earlier days is that it was formed before I knew what it felt like to be pushed to the wall. I hadn't yet begun to suspect that spiritual fruits such as peace and joy are not only bigger than the happenings of our lives but also bigger than the feelings of our lives.

The biblical "joy" goes far beyond the agreeably happy meanings we usually associate with the term. Such joy is inde-pendent of the emotional high we experience when we have a good day, just as it cannot be compromised by the emotional lows of bad days. Lewis comes closest to describing this almost indescribable experience in *Surprised by Joy*, an autobiographical account of his early life. There he portrays joy as something of a delicious phantom, appearing unexpectedly, eluding capture or even a very close observation, and momentarily touching its for-tunate host with a hungry longing little short of an ache.

Lewis spent the better part of his youth in pursuit of that touch of divinity, only to find that joy was not an end but, rather, a means. He learned joy was a lovely messenger sent to remind God's children that this enchanting beauty is but the barest hint of the Father's presence, like the longing created by a wisp of perfume left by a lover who passed this way only moments ago.

There are hints of this visitor in most cultures, histories, and religions the world has known. The capacity for joy is one of those pieces of the Creator unfailingly built into us all. But we often twist it or, more commonly, ignore it. And when, on occasion, it manages to stab into our lives, we are more likely to duck than enjoy it. The thing is vaguely uncomfortable and entirely untrustworthy. Better to stick with proven articles of transitory happiness like job promotions, new houses, successful churches, and healthy children.

And yet. . . .

There is a tattered piece of drawing paper which hangs on my bulletin board at work. On it are the clumsy block letters of a first-grader, tumbling into each other in a parade of sudden spaces and squeezes. I have not the faintest idea where my daughter, Kathi, picked up this little verse.

> Time to hang the holly wreath,
> and trim the Christmas
> tree, and decorate the hearth
> and home with love and harmony.

Something about that ragged piece of paper captures the full poignancy of both childhood and Christmas, as if every fond memory of my little girl and every Courier and Ives vision of Christmas has been loaded into those few, gangly words from my daughter's hand. I cannot look at it without feeling a rush of emotions—sadness for times forever gone, happiness for memories forever present, love for the child of my youth, and an aching hunger for a fleeting something which dances spectrally among the words on the torn sheet, but always skips away before I can get it properly sighted in the crosshairs of my mind.

The feelings the verse produces are not always happy ones. On days when I am brooding about Kathi's departure for college, now imminent, I dare not even glance at the verse. Yet even then I do not for a moment doubt that here is a curious link with the divine, a rickety bridge reaching out into a fog bank and anchored to some far shore I cannot quite see. Here is joy, the great messenger, pointing to God.

Joy can wear other faces. One is the exhilaration which

accompanies the touch of God. Is there a sweeter feeling than the awareness that, for the moment, at least, you are directly in the line of fire of God's blessings? But the danger in this is the powerful temptation to confuse the result, the blessing, with joy itself. It is the touch of God, whether resulting in comfort or discomfort, which brings the sweet throb of joy. We drink the wine of success to a point of intoxication, having long-since forgotten the reason for the celebration. But as the hauntingly quiet words of Gibran affirm, pain is no less a gift from God than happiness.

> And could you keep your heart in wonder at the daily miracles of your life, your pain would not seem less wondrous than your joy. . . . And you would watch with serenity through the winters of your grief.[26]

If peace means something more than the mere absence of depression and anxiety, then joy must mean something more than the mere presence of exhilaration.

It should come as no surprise that the waters of pain and joy may be drawn from the same well. Paradoxes are sprinkled through the Christian faith. Perhaps the three greatest paradoxes of Jesus' teachings are that masters are made only through serving, receiving comes only through giving, and life begins only after it is put to death. What seem like opposite ends of a straight line to us are, from God's perspective, the beginning and end points of a circle which, of course, touch each other.

Occasionally we trip over these kinds of truths. The cures for diseases are often found in strains of the offending viruses. Backfires are an effective means for fighting forest fires. Recently the medical community has made use of this principle in the treatment of anxiety through "paradoxical treatment." This approach suggests to patients that they try to enjoy at least some of the feelings associated with anxiety. Perhaps these feelings are not simply inherently painful, and can be appreciated in the same way we find pleasure in many new experiences. Perhaps dislocated fear, like anger before it, is an emotion for which we may find some redeeming value.

I confess I have not had much success with paradoxical treatment. On tough days I am climbing rugged mountains, not frolicking in lush valleys. My eyes are feverishly searching for sources of comfort, hope, and perspective, anything that will allow me a toehold in the craggy rocks. I see nothing remotely courteous, much less friendly, in the prospect. But this may well be a reflection of my weakness rather than the nature of anxiety.

☾

Time, nature's great balm, sometimes demonstrates a unique capacity for revealing the link between pain and joy. Looking back on a time in life which then seemed an unmitigated hell, we become nostalgic about the stabs of light which were God's only means of brightening our black world. One of the Creator's most loving gifts to us is the natural tendency for bad memories to fade over the years while the good ones brighten.

A young wife and teacher at our Christian school spent a year in tense anguish when her husband, father of a young child, fell seriously ill. A mysterious brain malady threatened his life and, sparing that, his long-term health. While Tim faced the torturous uncertainties and physical pain of the ordeal, his wife, Mara Jo, faced many of these stressors plus the tremendous emotional burden of having to carry on with her family, job, and Tim's convalescence.

For a harrowing year, Mara Jo had no way of knowing if this was to forever be her allotted portion in life. Eventually Tim's health returned, and they now live what most people would describe as a good life, one which includes three more children.

But Mara Jo recently made a most unlikely observation as she thought back on that time. Wistfully she said she missed the daily sweetness of God's closeness, which she felt on even the worst of those days. She was saying that this particular kind of joy seemed exclusively reserved for that particular level of pain, as if God meant the two to be linked in cause-and-effect fashion.

Little Much Afraid, cowardly cripple in Hurnard's allegory, learned the same lesson on her journey to the mountaintops of joy. Her companions on that journey, repulsive to the touch but possessing a strength which literally carried her up the steepest places, were Suffering and Sorrow.[27]

The point is dramatically reaffirmed by Darlene Diebler Rose. As a young missionary, Rose was trapped on New Guinea when the Japanese threw a net of steel over the Western Pacific after Pearl Harbor. It seems inconceivable that she could have survived the three-year ordeal, physically or emotionally. Her world became an unending sojourn through forced labor, flies, torture, malnutrition, maggots, rats, brainwashing, and the hovering specter of her own death. During her internment, Rose learned of the death of her young missionary husband, as well as of the aging doctor who headed the mission work. Every shred of hope and encouragement was ripped from her grasp, except one—the belief that her God had not abandoned her.

Interestingly, her very worst time came not during her physical agonies, or with the news of her husband's death, or even when she saw a Japanese soldier, sword drawn, mere seconds from beheading her. Worst were the six harrowing days and nights following her near execution, when she gave way to the battering ram of fear and, like Paul, despaired of life itself.

Only someone who has suffered similar raging fires can understand how undefinable fears could undo Darlene's courage when specific threats and brutality could not. Those six terrible days, she said, were the only time she felt lost.

Yet she would not remove even that grimmest of weeks from her memory if it meant surrendering her memories of God's closeness during that time. Looking back, she finds an aching sweetness in those dark days. God's joy not only carried with it a strength greater than all the sadistically vile possibilities which could have befallen her. God's joy actually took root and grew in the soil of her exceptional pain. Darlene Rose, without saying so directly, was reiterating the ancient paradox: if she had not experienced the pain, she could not have experienced the joy.[28]

℃

Robert J. Owens of the Emmanuel School of Religion has brought a similar explanation to the strange nocturnal encounter between Jacob and the angel. Because Jacob cheated his brother Esau of his birthright at Isaac's death, he is justifiably worried when he hears Esau intends to greet Jacob's homecoming, after twenty years, with a party of 400 men.

Jacob prays fervently for protection, but his only answer is the more-than-mortal visitor who attacks him. They wrestle through the night, but to no apparent decision or purpose. Jacob seems to have drawn a poor tie, receiving a dislocated thigh and a new name for his troubles. The former would heal, while the latter ("Israel") only confirmed that Jacob had stood up to God, a fact painfully apparent to him already.

But Owens infers much more from the odd exchange. The divine "man" with whom Jacob wrestled made Jacob face his dishonesty (the name the man forced him to say, "Jacob," means "cheater"). The man also made Jacob fight rather than flee. In this way, God forced Jacob to become capable of dealing with Esau or any of the other problems waiting in the wings for God's newly chosen people.

Owens finds "wonderful irony" in the fact that a crippling assault would result in a stronger Jacob, and "that out of the terror and pain of an awesome struggle, he came into his own, having a blessing that *truly* belonged to him." It is doubtful Jacob believed it was a blessing at the time, just as the terrible emptiness of anxiety and depression seems an odd gift from the hands of a loving God. But, as Owens says, "This is because God is more concerned with what we become than what we want." Owens concludes,

> What I am saying is that some terribly trying experience in your life, in which you have to fight with everything you have to stay afloat, may very well, viewed from God's perspective, be an opportunity for you to discover new truth and be made by Him into a more whole person. Such 'wrestlings with God' may leave you scarred superficially. But the reality of such scars, such limping, need not obscure the fact that a great new level of spiritual health resulted.[29]

These words jump out at anyone who has suffered anxiety or depression: "fight with everything you have to stay afloat," "scarred," "limping." But if the description fits, why not the promise as well?

℃

The Furies of pain have hounded Tim Hansel for over a decade yet have only convinced him that he is alive, that life is precious, and that joy is the inevitable reward of those who honor these truths. Pain and joy, he says, are "invisible partners" which "actually synergize each other." Quoting Clyde Reed, Hansel states that "when we cut ourselves off from pain we cut ourselves off from joy." This is the final leg of the journey which winds through the realizations that pain and joy are more than opposites, more than neutrals, more than compatibles, more than supplementals.

Pain and joy actually *feed* off each other to create a piece of life which is larger than the sum of the parts.[30] It is a chemical combination of sorts, in which neither of the two elements could produce the same result without the other, just as neither sodium nor chloride, by itself, could enrich the flavor of our food in the form of salt.

This also completes a quantum leap in our faith, should we choose to take it. Joy is a precious biblical pearl, always described in glowing terms and at least once recognized as the real source of our strength. It is one thing to say that joy can be had in spite of our pain, but quite another to say that it cannot be had without that pain.

Suffering and Sorrow were Much Afraid's guides up the mountain not because the Shepherd thought they happened to suit her, but because they were the only two guides in the mountain climbing business. All of the others—Happiness, Health, Fortune—would have turned tail at the first sight of a steep slope or one of Much Afraid's many enemies.

Scripture itself, says Hansel, gives evidence of this, for most of the Bible was written from some position of difficulty. From Abraham's difficult call in Genesis, to the bright visions of an exiled John in Revelation, we are treated to an almost ceaseless procession of agonies, including every kind of tragedy which can befall men and women. Yet this unlikely script produced the play which gave hope, love, and joy to the world. Here was no accident.[31]

There is danger in this game. If joy and pain are inseparable, what happens to those vast multitudes who try to separate them? I once heard a sermon in which the minister, wanting to awaken his listeners to the beautiful possibilities God has in store for them just over the horizon, said that if the proverbial Ugly Duckling had lived in today's world, where many counselors treat pain as an abstract enemy, he would never have grown into a beautiful swan. He would have simply learned how to cope with being an ugly duckling.

How many people are only coping with their pain, huddling in shadows, licking their wounds, their eyes continuously casting about for anything else which might hurt them?

Coping. What a hideously hopeless word. It carries with it a strong sense of resignation, an unmistakable message that since your present difficulty will not go away, you might as well learn to live with it. Is this a message to equate with healing? Is it the best our faith can do? Who among us would docilely accept a doctor's verdict that we simply had to learn to live with the flu, a cold, or a headache—forever?

Coping also connotes a sense of narrowness in which everything is reduced to easily defined limits. Suffering is nothing more than pain, medication is nothing more than chemical alterations in the body, and counseling is nothing more than the linking of causes and effects wholly limited to the confines of our physical world. Pain serves no purpose other than obedience to natural and predictable laws of causation, and we serve no better purpose than to escape it or defer it. Talk of redeeming it or welcoming it is absurd.

Perhaps worst, "coping" implies that our pain is entirely capricious. It hints that our best coping mechanism in this life is a shrug of the shoulders and a reiteration of Jesus' seemingly offhand observation that the rain falls on the good and the evil alike (Matt. 5:45).

For many of my adult years, I accepted this convenient belief. It was a strange odyssey which led me to the conclusion that pain and joy are blood relatives. The route was a circular one, ending close to the spot where it began many years ago, in what I had always assumed was my naive youth. Like most children, I was firmly convinced that pain was bad. This left me with one of two possibilities for explaining why things hurt me: either the pain was caused by someone who was bad, or it was caused by someone good as punishment for something bad I had done. In temporal terms, a bully fit the first bill, my parents the second. Extending my logic to cosmic dimensions brought Satan and God into those roles.

Time and education changed all of that. The disciplinarian God of my youth gave way to a mushy, "I-wouldn't-hurt-a-flea" God of early adulthood, a transition I happily supposed paralleled the metamorphosis God imposed on himself in graduating from the Old to the New Testament. I had only pity and disgust for people who tried to explain their problems in terms of God's dissatisfaction with them. Satan was equally ludicrous as a too-convenient strawdog.

Bad things happened because, well, just because they happened, that's all. Only an uneducated and unsophisticated mind would try to force the happenings of our lives into a morality play in which God and Satan played tug-of-war with the human actors. Such was not even an improvement on the Greeks.

But, at the high risk of repeating myself, that was before I experienced real pain. It is one thing to abstractly hypothesize about someone else's pain. It is quite another thing to make sense of your own. Once you have tasted life-threatening torment, the kind which raises in your mind serious doubts about your chances for survival, you can never again accept agony as something static or arbitrary. It must be moving, or moving you, in some direction, whether good or ill. The only thing you cannot accept, and still retain your sanity, is that something this excruciating has no meaning at all.

This brings me closer to the views of my childhood than of later years. For the issue is not whether God or Satan wins the war of the thunderbolts—neither should be blamed for or credited with leukemia, tornadoes, or the lottery—but rather how well each works within the laws for our world God set in motion long ago.

Hence Christ's comment about the randomness of the rains. Where God would have you see the possibilities for growth and refreshment in the rain, Satan would crowd your mind with fears of sickness and images of drowning children. But if Satan cannot get you to buy these images, he will be equally pleased to convince you that rain has no significance at all. Indeed, this is probably his first preference. The only thing more godlessly cruel than suffering at the hands of a readily identified evil is suffering for no identifiable reason at all.

☾

The separation of pain from its meaning is worse than foolish; it is ultimately self-destructive. Our cultural tendency toward cowardice, far from relieving our pain, more often compounds it—as surely as a child's tooth pain is compounded by an overly sensitive mother who yields to the child's terrified resistance to dental work.

Recently the antidepressant I have been taking, Imipramine, has been causing many side-effects. I have experienced dizziness, discomforting changes in body temperature (both icy extremities and the tendency to sweat), dryness of mouth, slightly blurred vision, some difficulty with urination, light muscle spasms, some testicular discomfort, and other changes. As a result, physical exercise has become more difficult in warm weather—afterward I cannot stop sweating for a long time—and I am having difficulty with singing activities at church, compliments of the dry mouth effect.

For several weeks I had trouble taking naps as light spasms nudged me each time I drifted off. If these side-effects were the sum total of the medication's dealings with me, I would be a miserable creature indeed. To voluntarily submit to these conditions without corresponding benefit would be madness. But the side-effects are only one part of a larger picture. Anyone who tries to convince me to cease taking the medication to eliminate the unpleasant side-effects will find me resistive for the simple reason that the medication *works*. The physical dues I pay to Imipramine are trifling compared to the enormous emotional debts I incur without it. Even if the medicine made me physically sick, I would prefer it to the mental blackness it alleviates.

But what if I received no positive benefit from the medication? What if these troubling side-effects were simply add-ons to my unchanged difficulties? In that case my continuance of the medicine would qualify me as a fool at best, and a masochist at worst. Yet this is much like what we do in our most common responses to pain. By treating it as evil or arbitrary, with no corrective or redemptive properties, we limit our contact with it to the side-effects, the part that hurts. We never allow its positive properties to be exercised. This is the worst of both worlds. We are guilty not simply of throwing out the baby with the bath, but of throwing out the baby and keeping the fetid bath.

Little of this discussion has addressed questions of "justice" relative to pain. What happens when the cure is apparently worse than the disease? What can be redeemed from a dead son? C. S. Lewis dispenses with 80 percent of these difficulties by saying that four-fifths of all human pain can be attributed to the evil people do. Most of his subsequent remarks about pain are aimed at that other 20 percent.[32]

Philip Yancey, who admits to being compulsive about this issue, agonizes his way through several books in courageous and honest pursuit of an answer. Perhaps the best answer—maybe the only answer—was one I heard a minister give to a despairing father who, wondering what possible good could come of his son's tragic death, bitterly asked, "Where was God when my son was killed?" The minister could only shrug and mumble, "I suppose the same place he was when his own Son was killed."

☾

Ultimately, God is a verb. We know him for what he does, not what he is. All around us we hear the relentless beating of his great wings, pursuing us, driving us, wooing us, lifting us. His voice is filled with alarm, encouragement, anger, and tears. He created light, loves light, and is light because light is the active intruder and darkness the passive resident.

But you prefer to slip out from under his watchful eye and into the dark shade of a cool cave. It seems safe enough. Besides, you are tired of trying to match his incessant activity and energy.

The demanding pest is at the cave's mouth in an instant—indeed, he ripped your shirt sleeve when you wiggled from his grasp on the way in. He calls loudly from the outside, half warning, half pleading, telling you that the place isn't good for you, that it floods this time of year, has no escape in case of attack—and worst of all, is a poor substitute for the beautiful place he has in mind for you.

He's been prattling about that other place for weeks now but you, in your weariness, don't much care anymore. You have even begun to doubt there is such a place. Anyway, you know he won't come in here—it's part of that silly contract he signed so long ago and to which he adheres with pathetic fidelity. If you can just hold out in here long enough, he'll probably move on and leave you alone. Heaven knows, he has many others to chase after.

He finally grows quiet for a few moments, raising your hope that he has left you in peace. You heave a sigh of relief.

Then you see the wolverine.

You might have known he would send that little terror in after you. The vicious creature is his favorite pet, for reasons known only to him. Bitterly, you think to yourself that this is a hypocritical violation of the spirit, if not the letter, of his precious contract. (Fortunately, you have little trouble brushing aside doubts about your own contractual obligations.)

The snarling wolverine immediately circles around to the back wall, all the while bearing its teeth, hissing, and burning through you with black, beady eyes. It assumes a new ferociousness once its back is to the wall, its only escape route now through you.

Some quick and emotional arithmetic temporarily convinces you you're still better off staying here. At least the wolverine is predictable. What you see is what you get. The animal regularly sleeps, wanders off in pursuit of females, and otherwise gives you respite from his sinister attention.

Not so with that one outside the cave. He's after you all the time; never lets up. And you can never be sure what he is going to do. At least you know what you're up against in here.

But that kind of thinking falls apart the first time the wolverine sinks razor-like teeth into your ankle. Before you can finish your howl, he strikes your other ankle, dropping you to the damp floor of the cave. Outside the other one makes a noise again, but the exploding pain inside of you doesn't allow you to hear him clearly. Besides, you have a few other details to worry about now. Down on the floor you realize you are in mortal danger from this tiny foe. His thrusts are too quick, too deadly. It is only a matter of time before he gets to your neck, head, or heart.

Again you hear the voice outside. Your indecision vanishes. Desperately you drag yourself outside. The wolverine makes two more savage thrusts at your exposed back and shoulder, sending white hot flames into your brain. But when it sees its master, worriedly frowning and crouched at the cave's mouth, it loses interest in you and scampers to him. Soon you are back out in the sunlight. The master looks anxiously at your wounds, then sighs deeply. A smile touches his eyes, but not his lips. Wordlessly, he turns you back toward the journey. You don't know how you can possibly travel far in this condition, but you feel the barest hint of relief when you begin moving again.

☾

Your joy is your sorrow unmasked.
And the selfsame well from which your laughter rises
    was oftentimes filled with your tears.
And how else can it be?
The deeper that sorrow carves into your being, the more joy
    you can contain.
Is not the cup that holds your wine the very cup that was burned
    in the potter's oven?[33]

—Kahlil Gibran

TRUST
You are not alone . . . .

Trust. The word comes at you first as a scream, then as a command. You are sitting in church, agonizing your way through an old favorite you have sung a hundred times—"Only Trust Him," or "Trust and Obey." Or perhaps you are talking to a friend or family member, trying to explain this terrible feeling inside, when they smilingly pat you on the arm and remind you to "simply trust the Lord." Sure. That makes sense. You have said the same words many times.

So you try. You push hard for the feeling of trust to come, telling God of your fervent desire to let him take all of your troubles so you can obey the biblical command to be "anxious for nothing." But it doesn't work. Real depression is not so easily discarded. Your fears are still with you. In fact, despite a lifetime of teachings to the contrary, you find that trust is the one feeling farthest from your reach.

Everything cold and brutal about anxiety undermines everything warm and comforting about trust. Since anxiety exploded into your life you cannot trust anything. Old pleasures no longer please. Enjoyable people and places now loom as threats, chances for disaster if you should happen to lose control. Habits, routines, comfortable patterns all give way under the crushing fear that you may not be able to trust anything to be routine or comfortable again.

Worse are the special times—the Christmases and birthdays and choir concerts in your life. Such times could formerly be trusted to provide rich feelings and fine memories. Now they are important only in their capacity to provide failure.

Too soon the thing has eaten its way into your most priceless treasure. If emotional trauma can undermine all other trusts in your life, might not your trust in God also be vulnerable? The haunting thought has no more than appeared before it burrows inside of you. You begin leaving your prayers with more anxiety than you bring to them. Familiar old Scriptures suddenly seem hollow, as if intended for someone else. Your mind protests that if faith means anything it should mean something *now*.

But the more you try to force faith, the farther it flees. Now your faith is not only failing to solve your problem but appears to have become the source of your troubles' energy. Somewhere deep within you a thin voice pleads that you are too much concerned with feelings, that the stuff of spiritual life cannot be entrusted to such weak vessels. But you brush this aside in your headlong rush to find some relief. Feelings are everything to you these days.

4

Trust: The Reach for God's Left Hand

Trust no Future, howe'er pleasant!
Let the dead Past bury its dead!
Act,—act in the living Present!
Heart within, and God o'erhead![34]

Henry Wadsworth Longfellow

"MR. MCBEEVIE!" Sheriff Andy Taylor says the name with a mixture of pain and disgust as he stands under a tree in the woods near Mayberry. In this, my most beloved of all "Andy Griffith Show" episodes, Andy has reluctantly wandered into the woods to confirm his son's lie—a series of lies, actually.

A few days earlier Opie had come home with a wide-eyed story about a Mr. McBeevie, a wondrous man who lived in the trees, could make smoke come out of his ears, and wore a belt with magical tools around his wide waist. At first, Andy is only amused, but as complications arise he becomes increasingly concerned about Opie's insistence on using the mythical Mr. McBeevie as an explanation for everything.

Comes the inevitable showdown, with Andy sending Opie to his room for one last reconsideration of his fib before punishment. Barney, agitated by visions of juvenile delinquency, encourages Andy to stay firm in this only possible response to willful deceit.

Andy trudges upstairs and sternly puts the question to Opie one more time. For a long moment the boy vacillates between his desperate desire to please and the truth, then he tearfully sticks to his story about his magical friend in the woods.

Opie ends with the plea, "Don't ya believe me, Pa? Don't ya?"

In one of television's few truly poignant moments, the agonized Andy looks at his son, nods weakly and says, "I believe ya, Op."

Downstairs, when confronted by the incredulous Barney, Andy shrugs and says that if you can't trust someone at a time like this, when there is no good reason for believing them, then what good is trust at all?

Hands jammed in his pockets, Andy drifts into the woods where Opie claims to have met his imaginary friend. "Mr. McBeevie," Andy sighs.

"Aye, did someone call my name?" answers a voice from the trees above the sheriff. Down comes a jovial telephone linesman, complete with marvelous toolbelt and a curious way of making cigarette smoke seem as if it were coming out of his ears.

Andy nearly embraces the astonished man (such overt expressions were nonexistent in the TV of the '50s). His problem is solved. So is Opie's.

But the problem of trust usually requires something more than twenty-four minutes and eleven commercials. Especially perhaps for one suffering depression, for whom cause and effect, the bedrock of believability, has lost meaning. The difference between belief and trust has been highlighted in a hundred stories and jokes. Among the best known is that of the high wire artist. As he is about to push a wheelbarrow over a wire stretched across Niagara Falls, the acrobat asks a member of the audience if he believes the stunt can be done.

After a thoughtful glance at both the wire and the performer's confident face the man says, "Yes, I do."

The tightrope walker gestures toward the swaying wheelbarrow and says, "Good, then get in."

Less dramatic but equally insightful was my daughter's first trip up the steps to the swimming pool sliding board several years ago. The steps themselves posed no particular problems;

the view from the top was something else. Even though it was a kiddie slide at the shallow end of the pool, and even with her father—still unstained, in her eyes, by fallibility—waiting at the bottom, Kim would not go down that slide. Her trips down the steps continued to equal those going up for several long afternoons.

All of this I found surprisingly frustrating. The problem wasn't the sympathetic snickers from the pool moms or the haughty, impatient stares from their kids. It wasn't even the silly sense of wounded family pride which accompanies such public spectacles. The trouble, rather, was the frustration of my omniscience, my ability to see ahead to all the good things awaiting her (positive reinforcement, a thrilling ride, a sense of accomplishment, and getting rid of the negative baggage that went with her repeated failures) if only she would let go and take that leap into the void. Her unwillingness to do so betrayed her lack of trust in both my physical abilities and omniscience.

The real problem is that business about leaping into a void. Leaping is the last thing fearful persons are likely to do. They might take the chance in a fit of anger or the glow of happy excitement, but fear turns them into a huddled mass of moral jelly like Kim, shivering as she white-knuckled the top bar of the sliding board. The tragedy in all of this is that persons immobilized by fear are the very people who, by virtue of their present wretchedness, have least to lose by dramatically changing their circumstances. Their fear freezes them into their pain. This is why I am bothered by that line in the old hymn which says, "Never fear, only trust and obey." Fear and trust are natural enemies. The former attacks the latter on sight.

Entertainer Dick Cavett, whose public image of smooth good-naturedness covered a battle with severe depression, hinted at the atrophying quality of that illness when he said, "What's really diabolical about it is that if there were a pill over there, ten feet from me, that you could guarantee would lift me out of it, it would be too much trouble to go get it."[35]

The cruel irony in the way fear blocks out trust is that the worst kind of fear and the best kind of trust both come to us from the unseen world. Most depression sufferers will, I think, tell you that the worst anxiety is not the fear caused by the big speech or entrance exam—tangible events easily identified as anxiety sources—but rather the cold, stomach twisting fear for which no visible cause can be found. Unseen fear from unseen causes.

When such anxiety hits the depressive person, no one on the planet is a more passionate believer in the *reality* of the power in the unseen world. But the game works backwards when it comes to trust. Suddenly, the same person becomes the world's greatest empiricist, unwilling to extend even a big toe over the line into what has to be a friendlier unseen world. Such sufferers will limit their hopes exclusively to counseling sessions or pills or books. They may, in the extremity of agoraphobic pain, convince themselves they cannot trust any environment outside of their own home. In so doing they guarantee themselves the worst of both worlds, doting with religious intensity on the unseen power driving their fears and dread, yet refusing for even an instant to acknowledge the unseen power which might redeem their trust.

C. S. Lewis' not-so-delightful Uncle Screwtape makes a similar case in giving advice to his incompetent, junior-tempter nephew, Wormwood. He points out that Wormwood can make his human lose both sides of the same argument over what is really real.

"It turns on making him *feel*, when first he sees human remains plastered on a wall, that this is 'what the world is really like' and that all of his religion has been a fantasy. You will notice that we have got them completely fogged about the meaning of the word 'real.' They tell each other, of some great spiritual experience, 'all that *really* happened was that you heard some music in a lighted building'; here 'real' means the bare physical facts, separated from the other elements in the experience they actually had. On the other hand, they will also say, 'It's all very well discussing that high-dive as you sit here in an armchair, but wait till you get up there and see what it's *really* like': here 'real' is being used in the opposite sense to mean, not the physical facts (which they know already while discussing the matter in armchairs), but the emotional effect those facts have on human consciousness. Either application of the

word could be defended; but our business is to keep the two going
at once so that the emotional value of the word 'real' can be placed
now on one side of the account, now on the other, as it happens to
suit us."[36]

What sensible humans would allow themselves to be so badly cheated; would, in fact, act as the medium through which they
are cheated? Yet we do it quite voluntarily and all too frequently.

To the Christian this is as unpardonable as it is self-
destructive. The Bible is full of references to the power, both evil
and good, to be found in the unseen world. Perhaps the best
known reference comes from Hebrews 11, which encourages us
to walk by faith, not by sight.

I recently heard a sermon by a Jamaican minister who
brought this Scripture home to me in an entirely new light. If
there is no unseen world, then the world we inhabit can be nothing more than a succession of nightmarish happenings broken
only occasionally by accidents of comfort or pleasure. If, on the
other hand, our seen world exists against the backdrop of an unseen world, then the latter must be of incomparably greater importance, for the unseen world transcends the mystery of death.
Against death, even the pagans and atheists admit to the inferi-
ority of our seen world.

For the depression sufferer, in particular, there is comfort to
be gained from trusting the God of the unseen world. "Oh, I
know," you say. "You mean the comforting thought of eternal
life in heaven. But that is not of any great comfort to me now."

I agree. I have found very little comfort in that thought myself, largely because anxiety and depression create such immediate crises. When lunchtime seems six months off and tomorrow
an eternity away, what comfort can be gained in thinking about a
shadowy, distant life after death? Thoughts of heaven may
soothe the wounds of a tough workday or a broken relationship,
but anxiety requires something now.

Slowly, very slowly, I am coming to see that at least a part of
that "something" is the knowledge that our present pain must be
borne in recognition of the importance of both the seen and the
unseen worlds. Your anguish is unbearable only if the seen

world is the only one which exists, if the way *you* feel and the things which happen to *you* are the only matters of consequence.

But the unseen world, which we cannot possibly hope to fully understand, may well hold a reason for your pain (and the less you understand your suffering by seen-world standards, the more likely the existence of an unseen-world reason for it). You are being asked to make this "contribution" of pain to the unseen world because you are not the most important factor in the universe. Something else is. The implications of this are difficult to accept for people who are a bit too practical or self-centered, both faults to which I admit. I know this is one reason anxiety finds such fertile ground in me. But like it or not, the logic persuades me.

Philip Yancey has written a remarkably honest book, *Disappointment with God*, which plows through 250 pages to reach this same conclusion. After examining the lives of several people who believed themselves failed by God during great crises in their lives (God would not even talk to them, much less grant their fervent prayers), Yancey resists the pat, orthodox homilies that God will answer in his time, that God will take away the pain if you keep praying. Instead, Yancey concludes that we must, in such moments, be serving some higher, unseen cause.

> The big picture, with the whole universe as a backdrop, includes much activity that we never see. When we stubbornly cling to God in a time of hardship, or when we simply pray, more—much more—may be involved than we ever dream.[37]

The spoonsful of comfort, then, come from knowing our pain is serving some higher purpose. It was at this point of awareness, and nowhere else, says Yancey, that Job was finally comforted in his anguish. Comfort did not come when he was blessed with new fortunes and family (could these have removed the agony of ten dead children?). Comfort did not come when his friends gave him advice, nor when he bitterly assailed God for an answer. When God did appear he still offered Job no answer in the sense of a cause-and-effect explanation for what happened. God simply reminded Job that, in Yancey's paraphrase, "If you can't

comprehend the visible world you live in, how dare you expect
to comprehend a world you cannot even see?"[38]

There was no mention of Job's return to good fortune or the
wager with Satan which had precipitated all of the trouble.
There was only the stern but eternally comforting reassurance
that God sees things we cannot possibly see.

This may seem an odd place to seek comfort. I doubt if I, like
Job, would have been satisfied with that response under similar
circumstances. Yet there is comfort there. It is the kind of thing
we must say to ourselves over and over, for saying it only once,
"I am suffering for a purpose known to God," leaves us with the
taste of a weak rationalization. If Christ needed to say it repeatedly to himself during his long, tortured night in Gethsemane,
then we can expect no less. Besides, the battle against anxiety is
best fought with continual reminders and repetitions of truths
which our fears otherwise easily rip from our grasp.

☾

But is this enough to sustain us in the crisis? Does trust's only
comfort come in the form of a thought? A truth? What does that
really do for us?

By itself, not much. It must be accompanied by acts of obedience, acts which may carry us right into the teeth of our fears. Ultimately, trust is action, not feeling, not thought. God can read
the hearts of men and women, but the ultimate barometer of our
lives is what we do. That is why the bothersome line in the old
hymn now begins to make sense to me, because of that almost
overlooked third verb, "obey."

This is the most powerful lesson I have learned about anxiety
and trust, for it was an action—not knowledge, or feeling, or
medication—which stood at the center of my greatest crisis.

My first serious bout with depression and anxiety in fifteen
years occurred in July 1989 during a Texas business trip. Somehow I made it through those long couple of days, after which I
returned home to a checkerboard pattern of "lows and lowers"
which depression sufferers (non-manic) will readily recognize.

In the midst of this dark battle the third week of September began to loom over me like a giant, steaming volcano. That was the time for my next business trip, one that would take me over a thousand miles from home for the better part of a week. Five days before my scheduled departure my already shaky world began to crumble.

Anxiety swarmed over me in all of its forms—uncontrolled fight-or-flight fears, leaden flu-like feelings of dread, the downward spiraling whirlpool of wholly lost perspective—bringing with it new reasons why I should not go. There were already several other reasons tugging noisily at my elbow. Wasn't it too soon (after the July experience)? Too far away from home (Why not try something shorter and closer the "first" time back out?)? Too demanding given the draining wretchedness of the past six weeks?

What would happen if I could not make it through the week? There would be nothing remotely comforting for me to grab on my way down; I would be exposed, vulnerable, with no safety net at all. Now, with the additional prospect of five anxiety-racked days leading up to the beginning of the trip, the whole venture began to seem a nightmare from which there could be no waking. It was the toughest moment I had ever faced.

This desperate situation was made worse by the fact that I could very well have canceled the trip without serious job repercussions. The meeting was an annual conference, not hard business. My only formal responsibility was to moderate a panel, a task I could easily have passed to a longtime association peer. Too, I had plenty of work to do at the office. And my boss was beginning to show signs of discomfort over my unusually heavy travel schedule. A stretched truth here, a white lie there, and I could have dodged the trip altogether. Unlike other separation experiences, such as church camp or going to college, the decision about making this trip fell to me, and me alone.

Yet there were two voices on the other side, sometimes so faint as to be almost inaudible, but never completely silent. One said to me that canceling the trip would guarantee a failure and probably put me much farther from a "healing," if that was the right word. I could fool most everybody, but not Lezlee, probably not the kids, and certainly not myself.

Historians record that once the Union Army of the Potomac began to retreat from the battlefield at Bull Run, after some initially courageous fighting, they gave way to a headlong flight which, for many, did not end until they reached the saloons of Washington, D.C. Along the way they overran the throng of women and congressmen who had brought along picnic baskets and blankets to better enjoy the assumed victory.

I wondered if a deliberate retreat now, before I was really beaten, might not have the same effect on me.

The second voice was more subtle yet, but curiously more arresting. It spoke not of strength versus weakness, nor of victory versus defeat, but rather of trust versus security. It said to me that for the first time in my protected life I had an opportunity to perform an act of real trust. With absolutely no prospect for a happy ending, or even anything less than a disaster, I was being asked to leap into the void.

Against a half dozen solid reasons for not going, this voice was saying that I should go for no better reason than that God wanted me to trust him completely. Here was no dried cliché from a dusty hymn being feebly sung on a Sunday evening. It was the flaming center of my life. If it proved wrong, I honestly believed (such being the high stakes of depression) it would ruin the rest of my life.

So I went.

I took my leap of faith. When all of the arguments had been accounted for, the one which held sway, and which I curiously managed to formulate in the negative, was that God would not fail to honor an act of intended obedience, however misguided it might be. All through that week in distant Key West, Florida, I was comforted by the feeling, which had to claw its way past my analytical instincts, that I was under some special protection for the duration. The feeling was strong enough that it managed to generate a heretofore unsuspected fear in the form of the question, "What if my *real* crisis comes when God lifts this special protection after I get back home?" Anxiety sufferers are forever what-iffing about some possibly worse crisis, a habit I suspect God finds occasionally infuriating.

The sense of special protection did not spare a rather difficult week, but it was less painful than the one which preceded it. The week thus served as a turning point in a particularly dark time for me. Best of all, it was filled with odd little happenings which convinced me of God's incredible nearness.

The point is, God did honor my obedience. It was the only time in my life I have ever been, in C. S. Lewis' words, "stripped naked to the bare willing of obedience."[39] Yancey concludes that such is the kind of faith God values most, "when everything fuzzes over, when the fog rolls in."[40]

Having experienced such faith only once, and having felt anything but courageous and strong at the time, I am in no position to brag about the deed. It was pitifully small compared to the life-threatening circumstances into which Peter and Paul were forever flinging themselves in violent acts of obedience. Yet, the difference is one of degrees, not substance, and the episode left me with a heady sense of wonder.

I now dared to wonder what would happen if I should ever recklessly throw myself into my worst fears. Are they, perhaps, papier-mâché monsters inches behind which are the open arms of the living God?

€

I am tempted to conclude I have said everything there is to say about trust since I have nearly exhausted my thoughts and feelings. The problem with such a conclusion is my first-person references. For if trust, my trust, means anything at all, it has to mean a great deal more to God than to me. I might, with a large push of honest effort, wrestle out what I believe to be my proper part in the trust relationship. But what about God's?

This is dangerous territory. Trying to look through the eyes of God may be like placing a two-year old behind the wheel of a tractor trailer. The positioning may be similar to that of the real driver, but the pull of the road and the skill expectations are so tremendous that disaster can be but a few feet away. Yet God himself, with his unfathomable penchant for divine humility, has allowed us glimpses of his vision. Part of this comes from the piece of the Creator built into each of his creatures, but the greater part was given as a gift in Gethsemane.

I wonder if the night Jesus spent in that lonely garden was more agonizing than his hours on the cross. The suffering of his soul that night was not distracted by physical pain. Worse, he still had the capacity to control his immediate destiny; he could still escape. On the morrow others would control his body and start the clock which would inexorably tick off the hours to his death. Then he would suffer pain so searing he would cry out against God's abandonment of him. But by then he would know everything had been settled. The crisis would be more of pain than trust. Gethsemane, not Calvary, was his great crisis of trust.

One of our serious mistakes (almost a heresy) is to believe Jesus was filled with divine omniscience during his earthly life. Surely there were such moments, in the desert or on the Mount of Transfiguration, but there could not have been many, and Gethsemane was certainly not one. At that moment Christ reached the full level of humanity. He was a lonely, terrified man, looking to escape death, questioning the value of his life's work, wondering where God had gone now that he most needed him. His cry to God in the garden was not unlike a billion others, and the silence which echoed back meant he would have to trust God on the same terms as all of us, drinking of his cup long after losing any good reason for doing so.

To assume he could somehow see how it would all end, with a vision of masses of adoring Christians and a church triumphant to comfort him, is to mock God's most remarkable gift to us— God's choice fully to walk in our shoes. Christ did not teach trust in Gethsemane, he learned it there. From that moment people would never again experience pain God had not suffered first.

In the midst of all such sufferings God's anguish can only be imagined. An analogy comes to mind which, while carrying the risks inherent in comparisons, gives me the best understanding I can muster. I see God as a father teaching his daughter to ride a bicycle. After a lecture on bike riding principles comes the moment of truth. The little girl is on the seat, as yet balanced firmly between her father's hands, thinking this business of riding on two wheels instead of three may not be so hard after all.

Then the ritual begins. The father runs by the bike, one hand on the seat, one on the handlebar, trying to simulate a riding speed without relinquishing control. The girl nervously jiggles the handlebars, overreacting to the pull in her hands. Her legs turn involuntarily in response to the artificially propelled pedals.

The method works well enough for a few passes around the parking lot, but it is soon obvious this is not the real thing. During a few more turns, the father lets go of the bike while still running beside it. This too serves a purpose, but the exercise is not true bicycle-riding so long as it remains dependent on the father rather than the child—and the untrustworthy bike.

At some anxious point the father realizes he must let her go. Perhaps she does not even realize the moment has come (better if she doesn't), but suddenly he is behind her, slowing to a trot, then a walk. With his hands shielding his eyes against the late afternoon sun, he watches her hoping her inevitable first crash will not be a bad one, and agonizes over her now futile cries for help. Somewhere in a dark corner of his mind are murky thoughts of shopping center parking lots, drunk drivers, and drag racers.

Yet even as he sees her veer toward that far ditch, a spark of joy ignites in his heart as he glimpses the first faint outline of a miracle—a couple of actual pushes on the pedals, an adjustment to the wheel which momentarily rights a would-be fall, the first squeal which comes from something other than terror. Such sights and sounds no number of scraped knees can diminish.

Now a new rush of thoughts fills him—warm memories of riding to baseball games on lazy summer afternoons, of racing down hills at speeds seemingly faster than any car ride, of the exhilarating sense of being able to reach places (even school) previously inaccessible to a child.

Even as he rescues his daughter from the ditch, he knows (though she doesn't) her momentary pain will redeem something of greater value, if she but persists. He also knows there was no other way. No amount of lecturing or running beside the bike could have given her the gift of bicycle riding. Action, pain, then more action is the only formula that works.

So too for him. For of what value is a doll's house or stick figures to the God of the universe? Dolls and stick figures know nothing of trust, nor of pain, freedom, redemption, or love.

SELF-IMAGE
You are not alone...

What are these feelings, and where do they come from? How can something this huge, this devastating, just show up one day, unannounced and uninvited? You are willing to be held accountable for your thoughts and actions—because along with accountability for them you have been given authority over them. They are, at least initially, subject to your control. Not so feelings, which seemingly swoop down arbitrarily, staying as long as they please, hurting as much as they wish.

Small wonder depression seems to have an existence of its own. Like a malevolent spirit which has suddenly decided to spend the day intimidating you, its heavy, anxious hands are on you every moment, its presence subtle as hissing hand-grenades. Even when you manage to be distracted briefly from its painful presence, you don't escape the leaden feeling. There is no real escape until it decides to leave.

After a while you become an unwilling but effective ally of this unwelcome guest. The very act of fearing its appearance—fearing the way you will feel—is enough to get its attention, often just when it seemed it was losing interest in you and looking elsewhere.

Worst of all, you never get used to the bad feelings, no matter how often you host them. Depression carries the unique capacity to be always freshly horrible. There are no veteran depression sufferers out there, coolly allowing their deep well of experience to ward off the attack this time. Each new attack carries its own one-of-a-kind threat, and each holds the promise of being The Big One.

5

The Crisis of Self-Image

He hangs in between, in doubt to act or rest;
In doubt to deem himself a god or beast;
In doubt his mind or body to prefer;
Born but to die, and reasoning but to err;
Alike in ignorance, his reason such,
Whether he thinks too little or too much:
Chaos of thought and passion, all confused;
Still by himself abused or disabused;
Created half to rise and half to fall:
Great lord of all things, yet a prey to all.[41]

Alexander Pope

THERE is a tense and clumsy dance choreographed on the stage of every human soul. It is supposed to be a waltz, but somehow neither the music nor the steps are quite right. Worse, the dance is attended by the poorest of numbers—three—and none of the three is content to sit out any of the dances. So they fumble around the dance floor, cutting in and breaking away, sometimes pursuing, sometimes pursued. They change steps in mid-dance, endlessly calling for a different song from the orchestra, but always, *always*, trying to lead.

These three dancers are feeling, thought, and action. They are as different as the kinds of dances each enjoys. Feeling is the

beauty of this ball and attracts the initial attention. She is stylish-
ly dressed, an expert flirt, and instantly familiar with all of the
TV-tinseled fads and gossip parading across covers of cheap
magazines at the supermarket checkout. Feeling provides a
preteen boy with his first fantasy, and an older man with his last.
At any other dance she would be queen bee, but the number
three does not work to her advantage. Occasionally her charm
slips a bit, permitting her two companions to glimpse the boring
mass of protoplasm lying jellylike under the sensuous veneer.
Too, they suspect she has something of a drug problem.

Thought is quiet, sensitive, and brightest of the three. Like
many sensitive people she is given to moodiness and worry, just
as, like many intelligent people, she is insecure about her intelli-
gence. What little humor and wit there is at this dance is sup-
plied by her. Feeling occasionally finds her amusing, even fascinating, but usually shrugs off any lasting admiration with a
shudder, wondering how anyone could be happy with so few
outside entertainments. Besides, she rarely trusts anyone who
spends that much time thinking.

Action is the strangest and least popular of the three. He
joins the dance, but more like a reluctant farm boy whose Ma has
forced him to come. He is ill-at-ease, clumsy, and wears the
earthy smell of the out-of-doors. While his appearance and manner are discomforting enough to cause the other two mostly to
ignore him, he is the only one who has never made a disparag-
ing remark about the other two. And were they to gaze deeply
into his seemingly dull gray eyes, they would see the faint glim-
mer of self-assuredness. Then they see that in his own element,
on a tractor or at an auction, perhaps anywhere other than at this
dance, he is somebody.

Rarely do we succeed in getting these three sorted out in our
lives. Even the emotionally secure among us are constantly
teased by the question, "Which is the real me?" Is it the way you
feel—those parading emotions like anger, fear, and happiness,
emotions which so often seem beyond your control and dependent on things which happen to you? Or is it the way you think
about yourself—that loosely defined sack of inner whisperings
which are forever reminding you that you are good at this, bad at

that? Or can the real you be nothing more than what you do, a conclusion society readily assumes but which few of its members accept in judging their own lives?

Not surprisingly, the "real you" gets easily and hopelessly lost. The dance hall becomes a dizzy blur as the three dancers continuously pick up the pace of their steps and the orchestra swings to wider and wider ranges of dissonance. Soon there is no hope for sorting out the dancers. Feeling, thought, and action—and who knows what other unidentified and shadowy dancers—all seem to have melted together, making it impossible to tell who leads, who follows, or who is who.

Don Baker, a successful minister and writer whose book on depression chronicles his four-year odyssey through that darkness, was honest enough to resist the temptation to see it all clearly after he emerged from it. Baker's painful journey led him through a psychiatric ward (the receptionist was a stunned member of his congregation who had seen him there many times as a visiting minister), contemplation of suicide, lengthy periods of counseling, and the loss of his church. He was pushed along the way by a blood sugar problem, feelings of failure, and what he perceived to be a losing bout with Satan after he had saved a man from demonic possession.

Yet afterward, when he forced himself to face the simple question, "What was the cause of my depression?" Baker concluded, "I don't know."[42] Baker was not denying that he had identified the causes—he had spent several previous chapters discussing those causes. He was rather admitting his inability to differentiate the roles played by those causes. He too was confused by the wild dance.

℃

In times of emotional confusion we look for the quickest and easiest answer. Among the three dancers, feeling usually supplies this need. Thought takes time and action demands discipline. But feeling can make everything seem well within an hour, considerably less if a drug is involved. During my seven-month struggle with darkness, a close friend would ask how my day or week had gone since we last talked. Early on I tended to frame my answers exclusively on the basis of how I felt, and so would answer "good" or "bad" accordingly. Even on days in which I had made some significant move toward my eventual healing, such as making an appointment for professional therapy, or forcing myself to complete a dreaded commitment, I could not see the day as "good" unless I felt good.

My earliest remembrance of a favorite book is *Uncle Wiggily's Fortune*. In the black-and-white days of the early 1950s, this colorful book was my nightly magic carpet ride into the images of my imagination. Through the voices of my mother and older brother I was swept up in Uncle Wiggily's anticipation of finding his fortune, which he proposed to do simply by looking for it. All of the adventures he encountered along the way were, I happily assumed, merely sidelights. They were merely something to whet the appetite for the final chapter which of course would reveal the long-sought fortune. I was equally sure the fortune consisted of some kind of material wealth, probably gold—or better yet, a pile of exotic jewels.

I remember being distinctly disappointed when Uncle Wiggily came to see that his fortune was composed of the many friends he had made in his pursuit of the ever-illusive treasure. My neat, simple ending would have allowed Uncle Wiggily to find the treasure while letting the friendships take care of themselves. Why spoil a great ending with such moralizing? Even as a single-digit aged kid I got the feeling that I had been had.

What I could not then see was that Uncle Wiggily was never really seeking material fortune. Rather, he was pursuing a sense of satisfaction for his soul (Of course, old gentlemen rabbits never put it quite that way!) and assumed a pot of gold would supply it for him. He would never have made his friendships had he focused only on his fortune. His response to the steady stream of needy critters which sought his help would have been either to ignore them, lest they take up too much fortune-hunting time, or to use them as means for his greedy end. By book's end Uncle Wiggily would have become such an ugly character no baby-boomer in North America would have cared if he ever found his fortune.

I am suggesting that as adults we fall, in our pursuit of feeling, into the trap Uncle Wiggily avoided. We chase after an end which is not an end at all. And in pursuing it, we trample all over the unrecognized building blocks of the real answer.

In our larger world we often recognize the extreme outcome of this kind of thinking. Drug addiction is the ultimate act of worship in a religion whose god is feeling. The crack user sacrifices everything for the feeling the drug temporarily brings. In the worst inner-city neighborhoods kids already know, without being told by the TV spots, that if they tangle with the "rock" their life expectancy is about twenty-four years. But some do it anyway. A few years of good feeling is worth the price.

Perhaps it is not surprising that people experiencing emotional duress yield to the same value system as that adopted by the drug addict. Feeling's charms are most alluring when we are weakest. But of course we never think of the matter that way. The upper-middle income professional, raised in church but now addicted to Valium while in the midst of an emotional crisis, still recoils in disgust at the sight of a crack or heroin addict, as if a chasm of difference separated him from them. His bright mind quickly rationalizes that, after all, his own temporary problem involves a perfectly legal substance. Besides, he does not take his medication for kicks as do those scumballs wrapped in filthy blankets and huddled in dimly lit corners of roach-infested tenements. His mind dare not toy with the thought that the two of them look the same in the eyes of the great seducer, feeling.

Ironically, it is during our prayers that we often fall into the feeling trap, for feeling can easily and innocently become the object of those prayers. There is a fading blue recliner in our living room which serves as the setting for my devotions each morning. (Prior to my year of trouble I never had much success in sustaining daily devotions; during that year they became the most important part of my day.) I could not begin to count the times I begged God to give me "peace in my soul."

The phrase sounded so biblically correct I wondered how God could refuse. But in truth the request was a bit of a sham. "Peace in my soul" was a euphemism for "a good feeling." What I wanted was a tonic, an elixir, a divine drug which would suddenly suspend those natural laws of cause and effect which had dutifully escorted me to this low ebb in my life. I wanted to get up from that chair and walk into my day with some good feeling about life which had graced my early 30s. I wanted to feel as I did before career frustrations, before mid-life crisis, before my daughter outgrew our need to protect her in our cocoon. And I wanted all of this for free, or at least very cheaply.

Of course, I didn't get it, and that sometimes turned my prayer session into a nightmare of compounded doubt and fear. It appeared I was beyond even God's help. I would have done well to remember the genesis of that magnificent hymn, "When Peace Like a River." The writer, Horatio Spafford, penned the hymn while on board a ship passing the spot where all four of his daughters had drowned a few weeks earlier. It might then have occurred to me that peace—God's peace—and good feelings are not necessarily synonymous.

If I was misguided in my prayers I could at least take comfort in having some respectable company. C. S. Lewis's torturously long journey to his Christian faith included a lengthy detour through spiritual hedonism. His love of joy was the only godly companion he allowed to accompany him throughout his life (and even then, especially during his period of atheism, only because he failed to recognize it as a gift from God). His love of joy led him to cross the precarious line between appreciating joy and pursuing it. Lewis found that he could no more capture joy by increasing his pursuit of it than he could secure a bar of wet soap by strengthening his grip on it. His problem was not faulty knowledge but greed and laziness. He was not seeking joy for its own sake; it was the *feeling* joy produced in him that he was after.

Earlier in his life, Lewis had been lured by the same kind of emotional fool's gold when he allowed his prayers to be turned into pleas for certain kinds of feelings.[43] Many years and a great deal of wisdom later, Lewis remembered his youthful folly. His memory appears in a typically venomous piece of advice Screwtape offered Wormwood in hope of subverting the prayer life of Christians.

Keep them watching their own minds and trying to produce *feelings* there [in prayer] by the action of their own wills. When they meant to ask Him for charity, let them, instead, start trying to manufacture charitable feelings for themselves and not notice that this is what they are doing. When they meant to pray for courage, let them really be trying to feel brave. When they say they are praying for forgiveness, let them be trying to feel forgiven. Teach them to estimate the value of each prayer by their success in producing the desired feeling; and never let them suspect how much success or failure of that kind depends on whether they are well or ill, fresh or tired, at the moment.[44]

Don Baker endured years of agony before he "learned not to believe everything my feelings tell me." He finally saw through Screwtape's deceitful ploy and concluded that "feelings, however, are fickle and often determined by physical conditions or external circumstances. I *felt* condemned. I *felt* unloved. I *felt* unwanted. Those feelings were real, but they were not valid."[45]

In our more rational moments we readily see how invalid our feelings can be. By the time we reach mid-life, for example, even the most immature among us begins to suspect that love is something more than the rush of confused sexual excitement which passes for "falling in love" among the young.

When our children protest to us that they are absolutely sure of the thing, and equally convinced that it will last forever, we can only shake our heads at the optimism generated by such bargain hunting. "Is it likely," we explain as patiently as possible, "that such an incredibly valuable gift would be granted so cheaply?"

And, though it may not do us much good with our kids, we are right. As Peter implies, love comes only after a long and disciplined journey through goodness, knowledge, self-control, perseverance, godliness, and kindness. When we finally do get to love we are gratified to find it is composed not of wisps of air but of stubborn, heavy clay.

Too bad we cannot make use of such insight during emotional crises. But that is hard to do when you are feeling especially weak and threatened. It is much easier to yield to feeling's sweet seduction.

☾

Thought and its impact on self-image also become some-thing of a minefield during emotional warfare. I vaguely remem-ber once reading a story about a knight and dragons which was decidedly different from the standard fare on the subject.

As a rookie knight, this particular young man had been ex-tremely nervous about his first dragon assignment. He doubted his chances of surviving. An older and wiser head, who under-stood that right thinking was a knight's greatest asset and lack of it his greatest liability, saved the day. The older man convinced the youth that repeating a magical incantation would make him invulnerable to all dragon attacks.

Whereupon, after dutifully reciting the magic words, the knight rode forth and slew his dragon. In the years that followed the knight became the most famous dragon-slayer in the realm. He was always careful to remember the secret words behind his power, and so he always fought with assurance that he would win.

One day he came upon a rather old and decrepit dragon. The beast immediately recognized the famous knight and knew his moments might be numbered. But what the toothless dragon lacked in prowess he possessed in cunning. He managed to en-gage the knight in a conversation, during which he both learned the secret of the knight's success and planted a seed of doubt as the real value of those few mumbled words. The knight was nev-er seen again.

Emotional trauma, particularly the chronic anxiety which can accompany long-term depression, works in much the same way as that old dragon. It beats you not on the plane of physical battle but in the closet of your mind. It suggests, merely suggests, that your image of yourself may be a castle built on sand, and that the whole thing might completely come down with one little kick at the base.

I vividly remember that two days before the 1974 anxiety at-tack which pitched me into months of emotional darkness, I was lying in the bathtub thinking how well my life was going. I had just gotten the job I wanted. Our little girl was getting ready to turn two years old (and another was on the way). I had success-fully begun my long-contemplated graduate program. We were, for the first time, experiencing the satisfaction of leadership roles in church. I concluded—I actually remember *thinking* this—that there was not a single thing wrong in my life. I was hitting on all eight cylinders.

Two days later we came home from a staff banquet at Jimmy Carter's Georgia governor's mansion (heady stuff, at the time). And the sieges of anxiety began. In the time it takes to watch a TV sitcom my life went from all right to all wrong. In some ways, I think the speed with which everything came crashing down was the worst part of it. It seemed terribly unjust that this could happen so quickly to something so long in the making. What hope could I have of ever again feeling safe from such a blitz-krieg?

Looking back, I see that the anxiety attack and subsequent months spent in fearful struggle were neither arbitrary nor spur-of-the-moment episodes. Much had happened to prepare the stage for them, including the unrecognized stresses of my life's transitions and my casual smugness about how easy life was turning out to be. But the painful time *seemed* entirely capricious and spontaneous. I could see no logical reasons for it. That is why it had such a devastating impact on my self-image.

During the ensuing months, my mind repeatedly entertained the fantasy that I would have been spared the entire trauma if I could have somehow managed to fall asleep early in that long night of October 16. Indeed I had come close to drifting off a couple of times. One less cup of coffee or a fortuitous turn of my thoughts for a minute or two, and I could have skipped past the pains of 1975 and into the pleasant oblivion of a new day. It was, I assured myself, all really a matter of bad luck.

Such thinking is deadly, for it implies that we are ever at the beck and call of chance, and it deprives us of the comfort of ex-planations which *do* make sense. The mistake comes not in mis-understanding the problem but in trying not to see it. The phe-nomenon reminds me of cartoon characters who have no trou-ble running in a straight line after they have left the edge of a cliff until they happen to look down. Any cartoon-loving kid can tell you that if those characters never looked down, they would never fall.

Not surprisingly, our thinking is vulnerable to easy attack when we assign it a role so devoid of substance and character. For if our self-image is no stronger than the arbitrary waving of fate's hand, whether that happens in the form of a wily dragon or a sleepless night, then we are all doomed to emotional failure. Sooner or later the law of averages will catch up with each of us, and we will be overwhelmed.

The mistake of this belief is that it makes our self-concept passive rather than active. As Screwtape says, "He [God] wants men to be concerned with what they do; our business is to keep them thinking about what will happen to them."[46] In other words, our emotional well-being is subject to the same doggedly consistent laws of cause and effect that work for all of life. We are not necessarily to places of tranquillity or collapse by mere accident or divine appointment, but often by our own actions.

This truth is at once both frightening and comforting. It is frightening because it rules out quick, miracle cures for depression and anxiety. It is comforting because those mysterious and seemingly invincible foes are at last cast in a light where we can make some sense of them.

This brings a critically important weapon into the fray on our side—the mind. A depression patient once described the agony of realizing that in this war "the only tool I could fight with—my mind—was the very part of me that was affected."[47] Getting the mind back in action is an indispensable part of healing.

I received helpful advice from our family doctor, whom I consulted during my desperate search for answers to my downward spiral of depression. He told me, "It took you a long time to get where you are now, so you can expect that it will take a while to get back."

I suppose I should have been upset with that remark—at that moment I did not think I could endure another day under those conditions, much less the weeks or months his comment implied—yet I found the thought comforting. Realizing that my psychological turmoil was the logical product of months or years of negative acting and reacting reassured me that the whole mess had come about because an ancient principle had once again worked predictably well. I could confirm that emotional disaster is not arbitrary, that my anguish did have some potentially positive meaning, and that I would have a great deal to say about where I went from here.

€

Feeling and thought having proved largely untrustworthy, we stumble to the third and sometimes least attractive of the dancers—action. On the surface, this partner seems dangerous, a genuine clod who will step on you repeatedly. Your dance with action is sure to be an embarrassment, as there is no way to hide that kind of open clumsiness.

The problem with casting your lot with actions in order to heal emotions, relationships, or anything else, is that we only half believe in actions. Or, more precisely, we only believe in half of our actions, and always the half which work to our advantage. The "do as I say, and not as I do" philosophy is far more than an old joke. We all practice it even though we like to obscure the obvious hypocrisy by lightly pretending to admit it. Ninety-nine percent of the men and women who have ever walked this earth have held others to standards of conduct (actions) they see as unfair for themselves.

Ask any small group of office workers on their coffee break about how to handle teenage burglars and you will hear all manner of solutions flowing from their deep well of righteous indignation—"Put their parents in jail for awhile," "Try them as adults so they can be sent to state prison," "Do like some cultures do; cut off a finger the first time they get caught, a hand the second time, an arm the third time."

Ask the same group about their tax returns or use of the company copier, and you will likely tap into another vein of indignation, this one aimed at you for not recognizing the vast differences between the two situations. "Those crooked politicians in Washington cheat me out of a lot more of my money than I ever get from them!" and "My personal use of that copier doesn't begin to compare to all of the extra things I do around here for which I get nothing in return!"

You will hear similar justifications if you ask about school discipline (as opposed to the unjustified punishment our child received from her teacher last Tuesday), and polluters (as opposed to our own fiscally justifiable decision to pull the faulty catalytic converter on their car). We want actions and accountability to come together only in other people. Our own actions must be considered in light of exceptional circumstances.

If we ever do favor the world with negative judgments about our own actions, we suddenly want to change the criteria for those judgments. Rather than seeing our grudgingly admitted bad actions as sins deserving punishment, we put bad actions in the context of our overall batting average. "By and large, I don't go out of my way to hurt people," and "Say what you will, I've been a good provider for her." Such justifications cover a multitude of sins of apathy and brutality.

In recent years a growing number of medical and clerical counselors have emphasized the importance of personal accountability—through *actions*—in treatment of emotional and relational problems.[48] Perhaps some of this trend can be traced to M. Scott Peck's *The Road Less Traveled*, which has made a large and favorable impression on the North American reading public since 1978. This work pulsates with the twin themes of accountability and action, as evidenced even in the chapter titles ("Responsibility," "Delaying Gratification," "Love Is Not a Feeling," and "The Work of Attention").

The first time I counseled with a psychiatrist, in the late summer of 1989, his initial insight startled me. He told me the most helpful weapon in the battle against anxiety is education. Then he gave me the assignment to go to the library and learn as much as I could about the subject. I thought this a questionable return on my $90 an-hour investment, but soon found it an effective prescription. In the midst of emotional struggle, when all of my senses were telling me this time I was in real trouble, I often was able to cling to what I had worked to learn about anxiety and depression. I remembered that it was not unusual to feel this way, that this was also something of a physical sickness, that it takes time and trial to make medication work properly, that there are understandable reasons for even seemingly incomprehensible feelings.

Perhaps my doctor sensed that I put a premium on knowledge, but I think that in any event he would have given me something to *do* in response to my troubles. He wanted me to know that the solution to my difficulty lay in my actions rather than his magic (though at the time I would have paid any price for some of the latter).

Medical research hints at the soundness of my doctor's tactic. Researchers at Yale University found that laboratory rats induced into clinical depression through uncontrolled shocks tended to escape depression once they discovered they could take action to stop the shocks. This trick was taught them by sleeving the rats' paws to strings, which the researchers could pull upward to hit the button that stopped the shocks. The very act of working toward their own cures seemed to help break the rats' depression.[49]

In a world where a mere wish can parent a thought, and a mass-produced drug can parent a feeling, there is timeless comfort in knowing that actions—the deeds we choose to do—can be good parents of both feeling and action.

TIME
You are not alone . . .

You know the nightmare. It has visited every kid who has
been to an amusement park or circus. It is the Funhouse Nightmare, the one in which all the amusements cross over the thin
line separating comedy from terror. The huge face which bulges
out at you from the distorted image in the mirror is grotesque,
twisted, and ugly. Voices around you are laughing, but nothing
is funny. You want to cry. Then you see the clown, a manikin in
faded red-and-white checkered jacket, slowly jerking his head
and arms in response to a motor which has given him life for too
many years. A smile is painted on his chipped lips, but there is
no happiness there, only the contrived, cracked laughter coming
from inside the thing. The seared smile and laughter follow you
throughout the dream, and even into your first few waking
hours. What madman gave this place the name of "funhouse"?

Time is something like that funhouse dream when you are
facing emotional upheaval. Time warps and distorts the passing
of your life until you begin to fear it as much as anything else.
Entire days, through which you once bounded with little effort
or awareness of time, suddenly crowds in on you. You tell
yourself that you must only live one day, one hour, at a
time—but then you see the next minute extending eternally out
from you. How can all the fear of a lifetime be poured into a single minute, you wonder?

All around you people absently plow through their time in
blissful ignorance of its dark side. They stare vacantly at the television for two hours, fiddle with a mindless video game for another hour, look at the clock, shrug, and aimlessly wander off to
bed where they sleep like a child. You envy their stolid existence, wishing you could borrow just a few of those oblivious
hours every now and then. But you know you cannot. This lone-
some valley is yours . . . for now.

6

Time: The Cruel Joke

Ah, awful weight! Infinity
Pressed down upon the finite me!
My anguished spirit, like a bird,
Beating against my lips I heard;
Yet lay the weight so close about
There was no room for it without.
And so beneath the weight lay I
And suffered death, but could not die.[50]

Edna St. Vincent Millay

ABOUT SIX YEARS AGO, at age thirty-eight, I began hearing a ticking inside of my head. There was no mistaking its sound. It was a clock, and its ticking told I was running out of time. Time with my children, the first of whom had breached her teen years. And time for my dreams, for the prospects of success seemed to fall off the table after age forty.

I could add other kinds of time which I was running out of (health, physical appearance, energy), but the ticking was primarily aimed at my growing children and fading dreams. It had never occurred to me I wouldn't be a father of children much longer, or that I might not be a writer ever.

I think I could have faced both prospects bravely enough had they suddenly presented themselves as *faits accomplis* one day. But any reputable sadist will tell you there is no fun in that. The idea is to string the torture out as long as possible, to see how many times you can convince victims they still might have a chance to escape their ill fate, like the cat repeatedly releasing the increasingly mangled mouse in hopes of enjoying one more romp across the floor.

For me, the game of cat-and-mouse was to last several years, and the cat's claws were ticks of that cerebral clock. Shorn of its theatrics, my problem translates into an easily recognizable case of mid-life crisis. Lost youth. Unrealized dreams. Resulting depression and its handmaiden, anxiety. All these painful symptoms did nothing more than put me into the same category with the 70 to 80 percent of American men who experience some form of moderate to severe trauma at mid-life. Such are the figures offered by Jim Conway, a minister who studied the male mid-life phenomenon after observing its devastating effect on many of his church members, as well as himself (Halfway into the writing of *Men in Midlife Crisis*, Conway's own mid-life crisis brought him within hours of leaving his home, family, and church in a cross-country escape.).[51]

I took little comfort from Minirth and Meier's statement that more sensitive men experience mid-life crisis at earlier ages than others.[52] Weighing the size of this compliment against the cost in emotional pain convinced me this was no bargain. Better to be a Neanderthal and put the whole business off until fifty-five or so. Besides, I found it grievously unfair that my thirties could qualify as mid-anything. I was less than two decades into my adult life. Time was playing tricks on me, I thought. But I didn't realize I was oblivious to the biggest joke of all—time is a phantom, a phony. It doesn't even exist.

Anyone who has experienced an anxiety attack will describe it, at least to some extent, as a crisis of time, or more accurately, a time overload. It is a nuclear reaction of your fear atoms, a geometrically expanding fission which pours unhealthy and seemingly unendurable amounts of fear energy into minutes designed long before the emotional atomic age. You feel as if time's obsolete vessels, these seconds which served well enough in former days, are suddenly too weak to carry the weight. It seems every part of your life has been loaded into your next second, and the whole mass presses back in your face, suffocating you.

The problem is not time, of course, but you will have little luck making that point with anxiety-attack victims. They see no way to make it through the next hour and yearn for escape. But the escape they seek is not from their problem, but from their idea of time. "If only I could get away from this feeling *for just a little while,*" they inwardly cry, looking for sleep or some similarly benign route of retreat. In college I knew a student who, after overdosing on sleeping pills, woke to explain to his psychology professor that he had no intention of killing or harming himself. He just wanted to escape for two or three days. He was running from time. But time was not pressing him. Something else was.

Minirth and Meier state that the difference between depression and anxiety is the difference between a preoccupation with the past versus future. The depressed person always looks back, saying "If only. . . ." The anxiety sufferer constantly looks forward, wondering, "What if?" Again the wrestling match is with a phantom culprit. Minirth and Meier give what I have found to be consistently comforting advice—live one day at a time.[53]

I sometimes wonder if such living isn't a critical but long-forgotten part of our makeup. Are we not designed to operate at maximum efficiency on one-day cycles, with our Creator arriving each dawn to supply us with needed sustenance and suggest what we might together do this day?

Part of time's deception can, like all fraud, be attributed to the father of lies, if Uncle Screwtape is to be believed. In counseling Wormwood about whether to encourage his patient to live in the past or the future (never in the present) Screwtape opts for the future. He notes that a large number of useful vices aim at the future—notably fear, avarice, lust, and ambition. Screwtape also counsels the young tempter to make good use of the troughs, or depressions, which inevitably come our way. Wormwood must convince his patient that these times will probably last forever, or at least longer than he can endure them.[54]

This irrational sense of the permanency of low times is another way we fall victim to the time joke. Even a child can understand that life is perpetual change, that nothing lasts forever, whether good or bad. Yet we allow our emotional difficulties to stretch into a black hole of time. This is perhaps the worst single mistake we can make while in the throes of anxiety or depression. Don Baker said that some of his most therapeutic aid came in the assurance of his doctor that "you will get better."[55] Such encouragement bears repeating several times each day.

$$\mathbb{C}$$

At most, then, time is nothing more than a catalyst of sorts, exacerbating anxiety to trigger panic attacks or suggesting depression will be permanent. But even here we are deceived, for it is not time but our *idea* of time which acts as catalyst on our emotions. The idea goes something like this.

Time is a great river flowing from creation to Armageddon. Behind us the river is broad and straight and can be clearly seen. Ahead, however, the river narrows and turns at sharp angles, offering only occasional glimpses as the sunlight glints off some momentarily exposed segment of the water. God, hovering over time and extending beyond its limits, can see all time segments with equal clarity. Someday we will join God there in eternity, where time will be no more.

I do not know where the "river of time" analogy finds its origin—perhaps in Heraclitus—but we would be hard pressed to invent anything sillier or more damaging. Time is not a river any more than a barometer is our weather. Time has no existence or essence of its own; time is, rather, the measuring stick by which we mark the passing of our lives. The fact that it is a marvelously consistent and accurate measuring stick does not endow it with divinity, only with a sense of mathematical precision.

Consider that old, troublesome theological chestnut, the problem of free will. If God "knows the future," if God can see down the river of time where we cannot, then our bouts with anxiety or depression are foolish at best, for no amount of worry or despair will change what is foreordained by the knowledge of God. And at worst our anxiety is sinful, for why not trust God to ordain a future which realizes our hopes rather than our fears?

The flip side of such reasoning says that if God doesn't know the future then his power must in some way be limited—which gives us greater reason for anxiety and despair. The choice made of these two traditional options will often dramatically affect the Christian's degree of emotional stability in times of trouble. Fortunately, neither option is legitimate. We don't have to choose between lack of free will or increased anxiety.

Like too many other arguments, this one has to do with language, especially poorly used language and the trouble it brings. We begin by giving a name to something we can't prove—the "future." We have physical evidence of the past and plenty of sensory proof of the present, but only our imaginations tell us of the future. Nevertheless, we charge ahead and accord the future full status on the timeline, perhaps because we are suckers for symmetry and can see that those three companionable timepieces—Past, Present, and Future—balance out nicely. Or perhaps we are suckers for security and simply cannot live comfortably in a story for which the ending has yet to be written. For whatever reasons, the deed gets done, and we now must live with this thing called the future.

Not satisfied with that bit of mischief, we make matters worse. If there is a future, then surely God must see it as clearly as we see the past—much more clearly, in fact. After all, God can do everything. The problem begins to surface here, for if God sees the future then that future must be "locked in" as God sees it.

Calvinists are honest enough to call this bit of logic by its proper name: predestination. But predestination flies in the face of the free will necessary for salvation by grace (We have to be free to either accept or reject God's grace; it would be meaningless if God simply programmed that response into us.). To get around this dilemma we victoriously proclaim, without a trace of a smile, that God knows the future *and* we have free will. If some poor soul dares to suggest such a thing is a logical impossibility, we pull out the ultimate weapon—we are finite beings, cannot understand the mysterious ways of the Lord, and so must take it all on faith.

I have to believe we can do better than this. Perhaps the beginning of the answer is that God does not know the future any more than God knows my sister Kathleen—because I do not have a sister Kathleen. Neither is there any such thing as the future, at least not in the way we have come to talk about it. The issue has nothing to do with God's power, so we needn't fear hurting his feelings by speaking plainly about it. As C. S. Lewis has said, nonsense about God is still nonsense.[56]

But it is worse than nonsense, for it is unbiblical nonsense, and this is where heresy begins to come in. Sometimes in our rush to compliment God on his awesomeness we turn him into a sort of musclebound buffoon, easily twisted into knots by questions such as, "Can God make a mountain he cannot move?" We think we do him a favor by forcing him into clever alliterative straitjackets like "omniscience, omnipresence, and omnipotence," but there is much mischief in that approach.

The Bible shows us a God who is forever demeaning himself and his power to get closer to his indifferent children, and there is nothing fixed or preordained about ways he does this. In Genesis, God carries on a long but losing argument with Moses concerning Moses' ability to speak to the Pharaoh. God instructs Jeremiah, already brutalized by his fellow Jews for carrying God's unwelcome warning to them, to give it one more try in the hopes that hearts may yet be turned. Such an order was little short of sadism if God was already sure of the people's final response. Perhaps most impressive is Peter's picture of God staying his own hand from ending the world, hesitating, pledged to redeem his promise of Christ's return but agonizing that so many should be lost if he does so now.

This is not the stuff of a rigid future being played out according to script. Rather, it is the dynamic tension of a living God and his people. The potential for disaster or glory is alive in every human life; it has not been predetermined elsewhere. Otherwise a mockery is made of most of the great God-people interactions in Scripture, as well as Christ and the cross.

The ultimate irony is that the River of Time actually limits God's power by reducing him to one of two limited creatures. Either God is hopelessly bound by his original act (creating the future), or he is just clever enough to see events before they happen, a quality not wanting in a few mere mortals. Either way, we now have something else out there—this "future" we have created—with a power rivaling that of the Lord.

I would not have spent so much space on this subject had I not thought it important to ways we relate to God in times of emotional trouble. In my own circumstance I have found that my faith has alternately increased my serenity and my depression, depending on how I view God's response to my desperate prayers. The worst days are those in which I feel a helpless inevitability about anxiety and depression, as if everything were set in stone and sooner or later fate would bring me down.

Indeed, the word "hopelessness" may sum up the agony of emotional distress better than any other word in our vocabulary. That is why psychiatrists and other counselors often begin therapy by assuring their patient there is good hope for full recovery. These professionals realize that loss of hope is a key contributor to the emotional condition they are treating.

But loss of hope is precisely what happens when we swallow the damaging Christian misconception about time. It reduces our responses to God to either fear or anger, the respective fuels of anxiety and depression. Under these circumstances, the emotionally distraught nonbeliever has a decided advantage over the committed Christian. Christians' ultimate anxiety nightmare is that God may not be in control of their life, while their greatest rage is reserved for the omnipotent God who seems to desert them or allows them to be unfairly treated.

Neither nightmare need be as unsettling for nonbelievers. Because emotional reaction is directly correlated with expectation, they are less likely than Christians to reach some extremities of despair. Their anxiety over a lack of control in the universe is simply a projection of their observation that people do not exert a great deal of control over their own lives, a fact about which nonbelievers had few doubts even before anxiety engulfed them. And the blame-placing through which nonbelievers' unhealthy anger seeks an outlet is limited to humans. Christians, however, with soaring expectations pinned to an all-loving and all-powerful God can plunge to deeper depths of despair when darts of anxiety and depression pierce their hopes.

Conversely, when Christians are set free to believe God can and will help them, and that their own actions can make a difference once they discard beliefs forever frozen in the concept of a prefabricated future, they gain an advantage over nonbelievers. Time now becomes the Christians' servant, rather than their master, offering opportunities instead of inevitabilities. No longer must they perpetually brood about a sordid past or fear a dark future, for God forgives the former and never created the latter.

God's great time gift to us is the present, the eternal present, which is only as long as it needs be—a year to struggle through emotional difficulty, a day to reunite with a loved one, a second to reach up and take God's hand. The only future we need to acknowledge is contained in the few precious promises God has vowed to redeem some day, at some hour unknown to us and possibly not even yet to God.

☾

Sometimes, the River of Time offers the false lure of escape, a temptation too powerful to resist. As a little boy, probably not more than three, I once knocked out the two front teeth of my brother's best friend. I was swinging a large stick (a clothespole, I think) and caught poor Deanie across the mouth. Worst of all, I think I did it on purpose. I vaguely remember some jealousy I felt toward Deanie's increasing claim on my brother's attention, and I remember immediately feeling guilty when I saw the blood spurting from Deanie's mouth. My mother tells me she learned of the "accident" when I burst through the back door crying, "Mom, quick, put me to bed!"

That raw instinct was, I believe, more an attempt to take advantage of the storybook properties of the River of Time than it was a simple desire to seek safe haven from my inevitable rendezvous with justice. No doubt I did associate my bed with feelings of safety and innocence. But what I really wanted was for the whole business to be instantly and completely *over*.

Even at three I knew going to sleep had a way of putting some things behind me, like a scraped knee, and bringing other faraway things to me, like Christmas. The idea was to ride the River of Time until it let me off at a more agreeable spot downstream. If I could just get to my bed, my time machine, and go to sleep before firm adult hands marshaled me back to the scene of the crime, then I could escape punishment altogether. Deanie's lost teeth would be no problem come tomorrow.

Depression insists on similar logic. It confronts you with a pain so horrible your only thought is how to dodge or at least delay it. God is trying to tell you that only the next minute is important, that hand-in-hand the two of you can walk through anything. But everything else within you screams that the next minute is the one thing you cannot endure. Somehow you have to jump over it to some safer place on the River.

If only a day, or even a few hours, could slide noiselessly under your small boat without your notice, as have thousands of days and ten thousands of hours before them. If only you could drift into some mindless busywork from which you would emerge five hours later with the surprised observation, "Is it supper time already?"

Sleep probably won't work anymore, both because it is hard to come by when you press it and because, should you find it, you fear waking to the terrifying reality that your temporary escape through sleep is over. But maybe some other distraction will work. Once, in the midst of a seemingly yearlong, depression-filled week I was crawling through on hands and knees, I was delighted to find I had just spent the previous forty-five minutes completely absorbed in my work. It was as if my resident kidnapper, momentarily restive in the squalid clutter of my house, had stepped outside to seek temporary relief from boredom. Of course, as he sternly warned on the way out, he would be back. But what a delicious respite it was. Surely there must be more.

(

If time is not the culprit, what is? If it is not the next minute which is unbearable to us during emotional distress, what is the source of despair? Satan? Death? Hell?

Or God?

It seems to me that only the God of the universe is capable of inducing this kind of fear and dread. Only his presence can waken, or rather reawaken, us to the brutal realization of our smallness and vulnerability. Gone with that assertion is the comfortable God we have worked so hard to create and maintain, he who good-naturedly defers to our cultural and social whims. In his place stands not the usual alternative, an old tyrannical grinch harping about commandments and punishments, but the God of the numinous, as Lewis calls him—shadowy, untamed, unsafe.[57]

This is the part of God we were not meant to see, not, at any rate, with the eyes of twentieth-century men and women. I'm reminded of Ebenezer Scrooge's trio of apparitions. Christmas Present, a hale fellow well-met, is an entirely comfortable companion, even when his message is not. Christmas Past, not unlike the raspy-voiced Ancient of Days forever reminding his people of the bright promise of bygone days, is gloomy and irritating, but he can probably be put off with a little bit of patience and luck.

Not so the third spectral visitor. Here is naked fear itself, raking aside humor and habits, drawing you to the farthest extremities of your existence as a living being, forcing you in a moment to see if life is agony or ecstasy by crushing everything else between them. There is no escaping his icy grip. Death itself seems nothing more than a formality, a footnote on your tiny spark of life.

As the specter pulls you closer to the dark shadow under his hood, you know you are about to peer into the awful mystery of life. Gone are the silly games, the familiar routines, and the pat assumptions about life and living which suffice well enough for every other moment of your life except this one. Now you will learn the real truth, and like the ancient Hebrews, you don't know if you can look on that knowledge and live.

This sense of "awe-ful" terror is not mere mystic dreamings dredged up on a gray Saturday afternoon. It is all right there in the Old Testament, partially surfacing every time a patriarch or prophet encounters Yahweh. We may, from the safe distance of a few thousand years, smile condescendingly at the animated efforts of Moses, Isaiah, and Ezekiel to describe these divine touches. We may view our biblical ancestors with the same enjoyment we reserve for the moment in horror films when the hero first sees the creature. We find it frightening, in an exciting sort of way, but the fear is simply a necessary and quickly disposed of prelude to the subsequent events. Moses is best remembered not because of the burning bush or sacred ground but because of what happened in Egypt, just as we remember Isaiah more for what he said about Babylonians than seraphims.

"Okay," we say, "that was a good part of the story, but get to the real meat. What happened next?" Yet I suspect the real actors in those biblical dramas never got over the effects of that first encounter. Every one of their subsequent actions was likely a product of the driving memory of the numinous. Their encounter must have haunted them long after their fears of other horrors—invading armies, persecutions, cruel monarchs—had dissipated, for they were carrying a vision too heavy for mortal minds.

No one can feel comfortable with this image of God. Our one hope is that God can bring us out of it or at least walk through it with us. The possibility that God may, in fact, be the "it" we dread is almost too horrible to comprehend. Are not love and fear opposites?

No more, perhaps, than joy and pain are opposites. And if pain is necessary for joy, then fear, even fear unto death, may be necessary for us to find the God of love.

It is insulation which drives this necessity. Insulation is the soft, spongy stuff of our lives which cushions us from the wild grasps of a rough but loving God. Historically, this insulation is layers of fat ecclesiastical bureaucracy, lengthy creeds, detailed rites of sacrifice, and dried-out repetition in services of supposed worship.

Socially, the insulation is a host of noisy distractions—television, politics, and the endless supply of news. Personally, the insulation is great rolls of drugs, causes, cars, homes, sports teams, and careers. It takes no math wizard to see that the passionate pursuit of even one or two of these forms of insulation, combined with life's physical necessities, will keep us out of God's reach for most of each day.

That, of course, is the purpose of insulation. Indeed, many of our best insulators are tucked in around us in the guise of religion, respectable R-19 rolls of busy church schedules, cumbersome church bylaws, and ponderous church board structures. Our frantic passion for busyness and structure belies our discomfort, even dread, at the prospect of being left alone with God. Far better and safer to keep up the noisy pretense in God's name, never looking over our shoulder. We continue to pitch babies off the back of the sled, feeling vaguely guilty about it but not daring to think what would happen if we stopped.

Only fear can cut through insulation that thick.

Once, 2,000 years ago, God, sensing our inability to look directly upon his face and maybe his own inability to tread lightly in our fragile world, decided to prostrate himself. God became incarnate in Jesus. This opened the door for untold millions to come to know God without having to be blinded by divine light or scared out of their wits.

Yet other millions fled and still flee to the safe ground of orthodoxy, institutions, and regulation. They see that this son cannot be trusted any more than the father. The son, too, is dangerous. He wants to rip away the insulation which protects and comforts us. We cannot afford to do what he suggests—all that business about lilies and money and such—but we dare not ignore him, either. Why not get the best of both worlds by making *him* a part of the insulation? First we'll make some rules and regulations, in his name. Then we'll draft a list of officially sanctioned practices for the church. Then, as for buildings and property. . . .

Whatever else you might say about depression, it is an effective insulation slasher. In its wake it leaves little that is remotely comforting or protecting. All familiar habits and patterns are disrupted. Eating, sleeping, and bodily functions become complicated. Challenges at work become insurmountable obstacles. Friends are shunned. Leisure activities bring pain instead of pleasure. Time transforms itself from friend to enemy. You are exposed, totally, to the raw elements of the universe.

And the only sound you hear is a rhythmic something you assume is a clock. But, in reality, it is the sound of God's breathing. Your life is being measured by the lengths of God breath. You must now find a way to live one-on-one with the only timepiece in the universe: the great I Am.

FAITH
You are not alone...

Strange that this whole ordeal should come down to a matter of faith. Oh, sure, you've always said all the right words and phrases, speaking at times movingly and with genuine sincerity about how God can handle all problems, that you simply have to give those problems to him. You've been at the bedside of dying children and young fathers where you joined families in fervent prayers for miracles. And even when miracles didn't come, you believed they could have happened, as you believed the miracles related by missionaries, ministers, and the Apostles.

But those were always someone else's miracles. Deep in the recesses of your soul—though you never dared say so, even in your prayers—you never quite believed such things applied to you. For you, there was another set of rules bigger than you and your games and your God, one which reflected inexorable power and limitless certainty, one which invariably operated to perfection when you were facing something of real importance. At such times you could almost hear a cynical voice saying, "Come, now, you've had your fun. Now it's time to get back into line."

These rules reflected inexorable power and limitless certainty and invariably keep the universe predictable when at last you needed your miracle.

Whether or not such rules ever really existed, you acted as if they did. During work crises you called on all of your work resources (God seemed oddly out of place there), just as a family crisis mandated family resources. Now you have this monstrous problem on your hands, this emotional nightmare. It is so brutally big it easily cuts across work, family, church, and the other little rooms in your life, leaving all of them wrecked. For the first time you give voice to your old, fearful suspicion: Is God big enough to handle this?

You doubt it. Yet the issue of faith won't go away, as if refusing to jump back into the neat cubbyhole you have maintained for it all of these years. You find yourself, for the first time in your life, praying on Tuesday afternoon, reading the Bible on Friday evening, and waking in a sweat to cry out God's name in the thick despair of a Monday night. Mornings bring no refreshment except for that which used to be a chore—the few moments in a quiet chair, searching a devotional book for some message which might give you enough to hang on to for one more day.

And you wonder, fearfully . . . how big is this problem? How big is this God?

7

Faith: Of Mice and Mustard Seeds

And not by eastern windows only,
When daylight comes, comes in the light,
In front, the sun climbs slow, how slowly,
But westward, look, the land is bright.[58]

Arthur Hugh Clough

IN THE MIDDLE of C. S. Lewis's *Voyage of the Dawn Treader*, there occurs an episode which, unlike others faced by the young seafaring heroes, results in no satisfactory ending except the sparing of their lives. Having sailed into a strange, dark mist on the ocean's surface, King Caspian and his Narnian adventurers find themselves in a nautical black hole which has the unique capacity to bring to life, literally, a person's worst nightmare.

After picking up a wild-eyed ghost of a man, who has been caught in the midst of this terror for years and who quickly manages to explain the peculiar horror of the place, each Narnian is struck by the vivid memory of *that* particular nightmare. All of them desperately lunge for the oars and begin a pell-mell retreat from the place.

There is no clever victory here, as with their encounter with the sea serpent, nor a satisfying resolution, as in their adventures with Eustace's dragon or the invisible Dufflepuds. There is only a wild dash for their elusive point of entry into this dark island. When they do manage to escape, their only concern is that no one ever again mention the place. When Reepicheep, the fearless mouse, chides the King about this inglorious rout, Caspian shamelessly cries, "You can say what you like, Reepicheep. There are some things no man can face."[59]

There's the rub. In everyone's life, hidden behind poorly constructed facades, is that ultimate monster which is, seemingly by definition, always a little bigger than the biggest good thing we can imagine. For many of us, emotional difficulty is that monster. When it tears into us all our prior, confident assertions about what God can do suddenly sound thin and silly. In shocked disbelief at the enormity of the thing we shake our head and say, "God can't be this big. Nothing is this big. How will I ever survive it?"

During my 1974 turmoil, the second of three periods of emotional upheaval in my life, I dodged the faith dimension. I was relieved and grateful that when I decided to talk about the problem with our minister he did not bundle up his advice in trite, religious fix-it phrases. I don't recall that he offered any advice at all, choosing instead to be a good listener and encourager. This helped spare me from a religious crisis at the same time I was having what I assumed to be a purely medical one.

It was probably good that I missed out on the faith complication. Any more breakdowns in my neatly compartmentalized world might have pulled me under altogether. I did not suspect it was impossible for persons like my minister to view a problem apart from God's relationship to it (whether or not they were using religious language to talk about it) because I did not then suspect God might not be confined to one compartment.

I would not, of course, have admitted to such an obvious heresy. Had anyone asked, I would have made all the right noises about how God is the common denominator of everything, cutting across all of other compartments of our lives. But I didn't really believe it, and my guess is many Christians do not believe it either. My God translated into my Faith, and Faith was a role in my life which needed managing, just as did such other roles as Family, Job, and Graduate School.

I had a different hat for each role. While I was occasionally clever enough to wear two or even three hats at once, I knew those times to be exceptions. I might have talked about God at work or in a graduate class, but only as I might have talked about my wife and children in the same settings. They were outsiders in a way, guests courteously brought into the room for a friendly introduction, then sent their ways. I could never quite bring myself to believe (nor did my actions reflect) that God should have been as much at home here as at the Sunday morning communion table.

I had much help keeping my life's compartments clean and orderly, often from other Christians. The "Religion Editor" of the local newspaper, whose very job was based on such order, was careful to confine his fare to the "Religion Page" which occupies the same place in the Saturday newspaper each week. For the uninformed, the page-two index locates Religion between People and Sports. But don't look for it Monday through Friday. The media's religion obligation can be nicely met on one day each week. Saturday is the perfect choice, because it helps Christians prepare for the day which, in part, is reserved for their Faith role. (It also helps bridge that little disagreement Christians and Jews have about when to observe the Sabbath.)

But the Faith Role has rules for more difficult issues than time and place. Years ago I was part of the church eldership which was agonizing its way through the murder trial of one of our deacons, who had been accused of killing his wife. The deacon's defense was being masterfully handled by a well-known attorney whose brilliance and competence seemed unfettered by the burdens of a Christian perspective.

We were asked to stay away from the trial. Only one elder among us argued against that advice, saying that at least several of us needed to be present in the courtroom to fulfill our roles as both elders and fellow Christians. He tried to persuade the dozen others that if our faith meant anything at all, it should mean something at a time like this. But his words sounded weak and unconvincing.

As a group we were much more inclined to acquiesce to the lawyer's request for our absence. After all, he was a professional in this business; we were neophytes. In other words, he was playing his strong role; we were well outside ours. It was all well and good to pray for the case from the safety of our church pulpit or the Wednesday night prayer circle, but we dare not take those prayers into an Ohio Court of Common Pleas. That place was reserved for lawyers, judges, jurors, and other high trump cards in the deck of the Legal Role. The Faith Role was nothing more than a three of clubs in such a place.

I cannot say what would have happened had all fourteen elders been in that courtroom for the several days of the trial, just as I cannot say what would happen if a newspaper reporter started writing about issues of faith in the middle of a sports column. I believe our church suffered a great deal as a result of the confusion and lack of information which followed in the wake of the largely unattended trial.

In addition to the support we were unable to offer two Christian families in crisis, there were things said in the courtroom which we, as church leaders, needed to hear. Because we did not hear them we were in a poor position to make decisions and shepherd our people concerning the traumatic events of that long winter and spring.

When Don Baker was suffering through the worst of his depression, it is doubtful anyone on earth could have convinced him God was still with him. Baker's Lord must have seemed as far away from him as his hundreds of powerful sermons, preached in bygone days in front of thousands of adoring faces radiating the bright warmth of Sunday mornings. Surely God had left him when those Sunday mornings ran out, gone in search of other bright, sunny faces worshiping *him* on *his* day in *his* church. What did he have to do with long Tuesday mornings in the psychiatric ward of a hospital? And even if God did bother about such things, what chance would God have to help, being so far out of his field?

☾

Theology only takes us from the frying pan long enough to dump us into the fire. The strictly theological problem is not, "Is God big enough for this?" but rather "Is God too big for this?"

The only prospect as bleak as being sent a ninety-pound weakling as a defender is being sent a muscle-bound oaf who can't even maneuver well enough to tie his shoes. Philip Yancey borrowed a thought from Frederick Buechner to express that frightening image of God's necessarily dangerous power.

> Without somehow destroying me in the process, how could God reveal himself in a way that would leave no room for doubt? If there were no room for doubt, there would be no room for me.[60]

Creation, itself, Yancey argues, is a self-limiting of power, a giving up of other alternatives.

> Every creator, from a child with Play-Doh to Michelangelo, learns that creation involves a kind of self-limiting. You produce something that did not exist before, yes, but only by ruling out other options along the way. Stick the curved clay trunk on the front of the elephant; now it cannot go on the rear or on the side. Pick up a pencil and start drawing; now you limit yourself to black and white, not color.[61]

The prospects for divine intervention get even more remote after the creative act. Where is there a window large enough for God to squeeze through without smashing down the entire wall? Of all creatures in the universe God is least able to tread lightly in our world. (God seemed to admit to that same realization two thousand years ago, in sending Jesus.) Lewis concluded, in a vein similar to Buechner's, that God's direct interventions in our world are necessarily rare, lest God trample the fragile freedom of choice which makes us human.[62]

The ancient atomists would have had no difficulty locating for us the trouble with divine intervention. They believed everything that has ever happened, whether microscopically minuscule or vast and stupendous, is the result of an original "swerve" in the free fall of atoms which began a cosmic chain reaction. Plagues and popcorn, the atomists argued, were equally dependent on the precise configurations of the bouncing atoms emanating outward from that original swerve. The prospect of an enormously powerful force, itself independent of the original swerve, invading the mathematically predictable cause-and-effect world of ricocheting atoms would have been abhorrent to the atomists. For them even the tiniest outside influence implied cataclysmic changes.

The atomists' logic, if not their science, is not without twentieth-century merit. Suppose the loving God we worship hears and answers the anguished prayer of a woman pleading for the life of her cancer-stricken husband. The miracle astounds the doctors, shocks his work friends, and is tearfully received by his prayer group at church. Most of the congregation, in fact, will have the story on their lips when they return to "the world" on Monday morning.

But it doesn't end there. By definition, God has now become not only the saver of a life but also the silent author of every act committed by that life until it be lost for good. Every time the man unfairly fires an employee, or takes dishonest advantage of a lawsuit, or accidentally runs down a child, he only draws funds from the account God himself has set up for the man.

How then does God now answer the righteous and anguished prayers of the fired employee, or the cheated party in the lawsuit, or the mother of the dead child? If God leaves the prayers unanswered, God seems like the capriciously cruel Greek gods who jumped in and out of human history at whim. If God tries to rectify the damage, he must make three more interventions, each of which will spawn dozens or hundreds of other actions, which will also draw their existence from the original miracle. The God of the universe has now become a cosmic Sorcerer's Apprentice, chasing wildly in all directions to account for the effects of a single, loving act.

☾

I spent forty-one years worried God was too big for our world, then seven harrowing months despairing that he was not big enough. Finally I began to suspect I might have the ideas of big and small hopelessly jumbled. We define those words almost exclusively in terms of two terribly shallow values: "myself" and "today." Anything which affects *me now* is enormously important and requires a big God to handle it. What is more, if that something involves present pain of any sort it deserves bonus coupons.

Two minutes of real thought would have convinced me of the foolishness of all of this. The idea that the God of everything is to be judged on his ability to play nursemaid to billions of squalling infants, each clamoring for different and often competing satisfactions, without consideration for the vast, unseen truths in the universe, is ridiculous and self-destructive. The idea is ridiculous because it makes God no bigger than we are; it is self-destructive because it reduces our hope to the limits of our own ignorant gropings in this world. As Yancey rightly said, there are times we must be satisfied with the knowledge that the seemingly cruel flow of events we call life occasionally serves higher ends than our wriggling discomforts.

The question at such times, then, is not how big is God but how small is God. Suppose we define bigness as what we can see with our limited vision, that particle of dust which momentarily flickers in front of the tiny keyhole through which we view our existence. Then there is a good chance the smallness we can just barely make out in the background may be the faint outline of one of the enormous, submerged continents of truth making up God's real world.

So I began to look for the God of smaller things. Little things. Two of these occurred during my business trip to Key West, Florida, in September of 1989. As I mentioned before, my losing battle with anxiety and depression had brought that trip before me as the most difficult thing I have ever had to do. I was especially distraught about the two bookends of that event—going and coming. I saw no way that I could have the strength to get on that plane on that Monday morning.

Worse, in the distorted logic which only can be understood by those who have suffered the twisted pull of emotional upheaval, I dreaded the trip home. My fear was that my anguish would accompany me on my homebound trip (when I should have been feeling awfully good). Then I would have final proof that I was wrecked beyond repair. Of course, by merely entertaining this possibility I ensured that it would happen. Even God could not undo such a Catch-22. God could not possibly be big enough for the job. I didn't consider that he might be small enough.

I boarded the airplane without incident or enthusiasm, working hard to keep the sea of dread at bay. Seated next to me was a pleasant-looking, middle aged, black woman with whom I immediately struck up a conversation. This was a long detour around my usual practice of being nothing more than polite to plane seatmates, lest they prove obnoxious company or intrude on some bit of reading time I had been anticipating.

But real difficulty includes in its mixed bag of curiosities the stripping away of such insulation. Because I was shorn of my artificial defenses, God could introduce me to Janet. It was a remarkable meeting, too remarkable in my eyes to have been coincidental, yet otherwise wholly ordinary.

Janet told me, in response to the most frequently-asked question among air travelers, that she was going to her mother's funeral in Alabama. Rather than just nodding or offering banal comment, I risked responding with personal and spiritual empathy. The result was electric. Janet opened the gates to a flood of fears and pain associated with her mother's death which had made the prospect of this trip sheer torture. It was, she said, the hardest thing she ever had to do. She could not imagine how she was going to survive the plane trip—she had specifically dreaded these very moments—yet now God seemed to have sent someone to her for this very purpose.

I was amazed at the tremendous sense of relief and gratitude which my simple encouragements (I don't even remember what I said) inspired in her. Over and over she kept repeating how good it was to see her worst fears reduced by our mutual sharing of her troubles.

I did not say much about my problems. It was not necessary. I could not have been better cared for during that trip had Father Flanagan been in the seat next to me. Janet was precisely what I needed and precisely what I least expected. She was also very small. I don't think God had to bump many atoms around to get her there, just as God probably didn't greatly disturb the atomists' eternal sleep in getting me there for her. Had I tried to tell anyone else on the plane what a remarkable thing was happening they would have shrugged and yawned. Yet I was convinced I had been a part of a miracle every bit as big as my huge need for it.

That left the trip home. There was no Janet for me then. What I got instead was a guy named Hugo. America's most devastating hurricane in a generation provided a darkly fascinating backdrop for my week in Key West. For a day or two we couldn't be sure that Hugo wasn't coming our way. A peer of mine pointed out that the highest land on the Key was eighteen feet above sea level, which turned out to be the height of Hugo's enormous wash.

But even after turning away from us and taking deadly aim on Charleston, the storm still played havoc with our lives. Flights all along the seaboard were scrambled, including mine. Once Hugo stayed well east of Miami, I thought my connections were safe, since my only other one was one hundred miles inland at Charlotte. When Charlotte went under water I had to take anything I could get, which turned out to be a flight to Dayton with a rental car ride to Columbus tacked on.

Perhaps it was preoccupation with the hurricane, perhaps the blissfully quiet ninety-minute car ride after a day in frantic airports and jammed planes, perhaps my need to be busy with thinking and planning all day long. But I never quite got around to succumbing to the anxiety I had so dreaded. Did God send Hugo to help me out of my dilemma? I don't believe so. (How could he have explained such a thing to his saints in Charleston?) But I do believe God pushed me into several of the cracks created by the storm. Just little nudges, nothing that would wrench the world out of its rotation. Anything bigger probably would have failed me.

☾

Paradoxes! God always seems to speak to us in paradoxes. Small wonder God's Son should have been known, to some, as one who spoke in riddles. Big is little. Little is big. First is last. But now I was faced with the most absurd of all paradoxes: "strength comes through weakness." That paradox was closely followed by its equally disturbing half-cousin: "to find your life you must surrender it."

As I looked around me, I did not see many Christians who were making weakness their goal. What I saw were Christians engaging in exercise programs, reading self-help books, confidently advancing in their careers, and otherwise strengthening themselves for what they perceived to be God's service. Nor was I much illuminated by the life of Paul, who gave voice to the first paradox. The apostle seemed anything but weak and showed little evidence that he knew the meaning of the word surrender.

Yet there had to be a reason I had been brought to the wretched state I reached in 1989 and early 1990. Somewhere in that anguish was at least the comfort of a lesson, some mere sliver of truth which could only be exposed to me under such circumstances. I could not believe God would allow me to suffer this way without offering some redemptive value in return.

I was not disappointed. But I did have to change a couple of words around before the meaning cleared for me. When "weakness" and "surrender" became "humility" and "acceptance" I was finally able to begin to understand this greatest of the God-human mysteries. Humility is the true realization of who we are, and we are (comes another paradox!) both little better than dust and little less than angels. We can soar for months, perhaps years, seemingly without effort and with an ever increasing sense of self-confidence. But just as surely, we experience times of spirit-crushing desolation. This too is inherent in the stuff of which we are made. It is not defeat, not really weakness, but genuine humility—the other half of the realization of who we are.

The fascinating part of this paradox is that our true opportunities for "soaring" may come more often during times of desolation than during long moments of confident self-assurance. The simple reason is that at our low points we are no longer in the way of ourselves. Once you reach the point of real humility, when you despair of pulling yourself out of the mess (acceptance), *then* God has full access to the workroom of your life. The point is not strength in spite of weakness, nor even strength through weakness, but strength *only* through weakness.

This makes sense only when we escape the limitations of the English term *weakness*. We most frequently associate weakness with a character flaw such as alcoholism or a hot temper, or with a lack of physical or emotional stamina. We then equate this image with the concept of humility. But this is more than a language problem. Our cultural idea of strength is equated with independence. Real North Americans don't need a dictator, their boss, tranquilizers, or antidepressants. They don't need anything, in fact. Not even God. Hollywood's leading male—and, increasingly, female—roles are still just faint imitations of Gary Cooper. Ask them if they can get along without anything or anybody and they will tell you, "Yup!"

Conversely, *humility*—recognition that we depend on God for realizing our full value as humans—is disdained. Compliment your bright, young, Christian friends on their humility and they will probably look uncomfortable. Describe them as "meek" and you will see color rise. Push your luck and call them "submissive" and prepare to enter a nasty scene. But distasteful as it may be to our culturally implanted sense of pride, submission is the heart of the issue.

Catherine Marshall, never likely to be confused with Gary Cooper, found herself dragged to the same conclusion. After battling a serious illness for months and exhausting her prayers of faith for healing, she finally stumbled on the answer when she gave up—on herself, that is. She described this as a point of "abject acceptance."

Marshall's final prayer, the one which worked, went like this: "I'm tired of asking . . . I'm beaten, finished. God, you decide what you want for me." This is not the kind of stuff to be thundered from pulpits or emblazoned on Hallmark get-well cards. Too bad, because her healing began the moment she whispered that pathetic prayer. She concluded her distorted sense of spiritual strength had been the problem all along.

> Through this incident and others that followed, God was trying to teach me something important about prayer. Gradually, I saw that a demanding spirit, with self-will as its rudder, blocks prayer. I understood that the reason for this is that God absolutely refuses to

> violate our free will; that therefore, unless self-will is voluntarily given up, even God cannot move to answer prayer.[63]

This passage does not completely dispel the gray clouds which crowd my understanding of a difficult concept. I still squirm every time I hear someone say, "Just give your life over to Jesus." What exactly does that mean? Marshall does, however, offer me a shaft of light. She at least leaves me in the somewhat comforting, albeit ridiculous, position of knowing that while I may not be able to define true humility, I know it when I see it.

I saw humility that morning I got on the plane for Florida. Stripped of all insulation, including that which I believed crucial for survival, I let go of any hope I had of controlling the outcome. It was no glorious moment, no thrilling affirmation of my faith. I instead experienced a simple releasing of my responsibility for seeing that things turned out right.

I was not quitting. That would have meant staying in bed that morning or collapsing in a corner of the airport. I went ahead, assuming disaster would probably strike at any moment, but no longer thinking that I could or should do anything about it. The feeling was a strange one and certainly a new one. My movements were suddenly a bit lighter.

That experience, and others like it, caused a few more somersaults in my ideas about strength and weakness. Through seven eternally long months I felt the weakest I have ever felt. Even without society's stereotypical accusations of weakness—the need for tranquilizers, antidepressants, psychological counseling—I was ashamed of my weakness.

Yet something about that conclusion did not make total sense. A simple bit of logic screamed out at me that, if truly at my weakest, I could hardly have survived the most brutal seven months of my life. Courage, I have long believed, is not compulsive action, which requires only a moment of emotional upheaval, the obeying of a quick squirt of Adrenalin. Courage is rather the willingness to stand up to danger, however limply, when there is no end in sight to the danger.

For my little part, I somehow crawled through some 200 days seemingly without hope that I could survive even one of them, and frequently without hope that the days would ever end. But this was no Medal of Honor performance for the simple reason that during much of that time I was not running on my own power. I went so low that I slipped wholly beneath my own capacities—a terrifying prospect—and so fell into the hands of the only living presence which separates us from total destruction.

My weakness had become my strength. But dear God, that was a hard thing to see at the time! I gained an appreciation for the sense of awe and terror which the Old Testament prophets always managed to include in their descriptions of appearing before the living God.

God did allow me to keep one crumb of my old meal, although I am sure it was against the rules. My most fervent prayer was, oddly enough, that I would be allowed to stay on my feet. No hospitals. No long retreats to the house or bed. Nothing that could be called a "breakdown." Some ancient, dangling thread of my once strong web of pride stubbornly refused to be blown away by the winds which had ripped away everything else. And so I pleaded with God to let me keep going; where, why, and how, I had not the faintest idea. But I must keep going.

I had no right to expect this. The state I had reached should have incapacitated me. But miraculously—and here the word has real meaning for me—I kept functioning, kept going to work, kept parenting, kept meeting church responsibilities, kept hosting guests, kept writing. Lezlee alone knew how close my nose was to the ground, but it never quite touched. I was a lifeless scarecrow, frequently relying on the cold, steel rod running up my back to keep me vertical, but it worked.

☾

At some point, in even the most mundane or vile lives, I believe God gives each of us a chance for our unique Possibility. For some it may be a lifelong calling, such as teaching or medicine, perhaps. For others it may be a relationship, someone nudged into our path who, unbeknownst to us, is the key for unlocking the potential of our life. For still others—who can say how many millions?—the Possibility may be no bigger than a brief moment in the sun, perhaps a class, or a gift, or some seemingly insignificant achievement which can only have much meaning for one life.

In the film, *Places in the Heart,* the African-American drifter, Moses, beaten and driven from town by the Klan, is reminded he has reason to celebrate. No matter what happened or will happen, he brought in the county's first cotton crop of the season, and he did so against the longest of odds.

This didn't seem like much and was dramatically unsatisfying for North American audiences which insist on nothing less than Rambo endings for the righting of wrongs. But for Moses it was enough. He had realized his Possibility. Likewise the Arthur of *Camelot,* standing in the midst of his ruined kingdom, was fulfilled by the inspiring realization that for the briefest of moments he had grabbed the full measure of his Possibility.

Romantic nonsense? I would have quickly concluded as much not so long ago. Now I can think of little else which makes sense. Among our very few certainties about human nature is the universally accepted belief that each of us is different from everyone else. Why? Why are humans created so mysteriously unpredictable unless we were meant to be unique containers for unique seeds of life the Creator planted within us?

Here is no theologically barnacled "will of God," no divine play which must be performed to the letter of the script. The loving God of Scripture would not saddle us with such an albatross; he would never be content to be a puppeteer. God's "will" for our lives is nothing more nor less than a hint, a suggestion, a prod. Were the word not so loaded with ecclesiastical dead weight, I might term it a "calling."

But whatever you call the Possibility, it is present in every life. You can see it if you look closely. I saw it on a night years ago when the rains were heavy and flooded our neighbor's basement. Our middle-aged neighbor was, I had confidently assumed, a rather predictable type. She was a bit overweight, loud, hard, and doing her best to cuss her way through the parenting of three rambunctious sons and a missing husband.

But that night, as I watched her pulling the wrecked refuse

from her flooded basement, I saw something else. Scattered all over her front lawn were paintings—her paintings—sad, soggy testimonials to the distant days of art school and dreams of what might have been. Somewhere in the tired resignation of her eyes I saw real human hurt, not the hurt of misfortune or pain, but the hurt of an unrealized Possibility.

I also saw it in a fellow worker, a bitter, lonely, remnant of a man whose life, less so than anyone else I have met, betrayed the touch of God. His constant screechings about niggers, Jews, liberals, and a long list of others who had managed to offend him might have qualified him for another century had he possessed any of the larger qualities of the Nietzsches of the world.

But in all ways he was a very small man, pathetically insecure and emotionally crippled. His attempts at an arrogant confidence in the certainty of science and the foolishness of faith were just poor and unconvincing imitations of other such performances he had seen somewhere. I consoled myself amidst his constant irritations with the thought that at least I had stumbled on something completely unique, a reasonable resemblance to a human being who had managed altogether to escape the divine spark.

But then one day, when he must have momentarily tired of holding his guard so high, he spoke in soft words of his love of rare books and glass. He collected these, in fact, and even though he later tried to give the impression that this was merely a business venture of sorts, I knew he never parted with some of these treasures. I knew he kept some of them only because of their unique beauty. I knew I had stumbled on his Possibility, and wondered if he might yet make something of it.

If he doesn't, he will have plenty of company. I think most of us miss the chance at our Possibility, in spite of the hunger with which God endows the gift in order to give it a real chance. But the hunger can, with a good deal of effort, be successfully resisted. Seldom are we a more gracious host to the Great Deceiver than at the moment when God is calling us to come forward and receive our inheritance, to make our Possibility into our Reality.

In the video version of *Happiness Is a Choice*, Don Baker states that while God deals in specifics, Satan deals in generalities. In the Bible God's anger is always directed at some particular, clearly identified sin. Satan prefers the less redeemable weight of free-floating generalities—guilt, fear, worry, and frustration. These he offers to us in generous supply when God, in the moment of clear revelation granted at least once to every human life, calls us to reach for our Possibility.

"It's not very practical," the voice whispers. "Things like that never work out for you anyway. Something's bound to go wrong, and then you'll be left with nothing," the voice says, warming to its task. "And just who do you think you are? You're not nearly as good at this thing as you think. You'll blow it. Stick to the small stuff."

Then the final assault, which ensures that not only will you fail to accept God's unique gift for your life but will also bitterly hold God responsible for that failure ever after. "Wherever did you get the idea that you deserved something like this? You don't! The Old Man is simply showing you what you might have gotten if you hadn't been such a jerk. At this point, it's all just a big tease."

And so begins the business of making excuses for missing our magic moment—excuses to our friends, excuses to ourselves. But the hunger, of course, remains. Like the fruit pulp created to nourish a young seed, it seeks to serve the thing for which it was created. The absence of the seed does not diminish its fruit value but it does drive it in pursuit of some other appetite to satiate. Inevitably, this twisting of the natural order of things leads, I believe, to hostility, anxiety, and depression.

☾

My Possibility has been no shrinking violet. It has had everything to do with getting me into and, just perhaps, out of this great crisis of my life. It also has had everything to do with the problem and paradox of my faith. In a word, that Possibility is Writing.

There is no point in boring everybody with a long harangue about my passion for writing. Those who have felt the aching summons of this particular Possibility, which even the blatantly secular world recognizes as the "Call of the Muse," will understand; those who have not probably will not, except to the extent that they can relate it to the calling of their own Possibility.

Suffice to say that writing is the only thing in my life (a rather left-brained, analytical life, by the way) which I have ever felt as a calling. Writing is the only thing I intuitively believed, at the risk of sounding melodramatic, I was "meant to do." I cannot say that about my marriage or my children, even though these are more important to me, nor can I say it about my choices of career and church. Somewhere along the line, for reasons known only to him, God chose to grace me with a marginal supply of ability and the Possibility of writing.

Like most novice writers (I dare not say "young," since I did not begin in earnest until I was almost thirty) inflamed by the possibilities inherent in those first written words, I assumed it was my job to dream the biggest of dreams. Multimillion-seller books and a moderately enormous national following seemed not out of the question, even if it meant waiting a year or two.

I was not blind to the audacity of this 70mm vision, but I justified it on the basis of the genuine hunger which drove it, and which refused to dissipate as did the pipe dreams of my life. Of course God would allow—actually help—me to become a great Christian writer; it was one of the few prayers I had ever made with which God would entirely agree. God's will and my will were the same. What a fortunate coincidence!

And so began the great work. Two novels, two novellas, three children's novels, starts on two other children's books, half a dozen short stories, and a variety of assorted prose. Perhaps a half a million words scattered over ten years, wrenched from the tired moments at the end of long days or stolen from odd hours when the kids were away. Not one of those words was written without first being bathed in prayer.

And not one of those words has been published.

At first it did not matter so much. In fact, I cannot claim it mattered at all, since I made no effort to get anything published for nine years. The kids were young; so was I. My job was going well, and everything else seemed to be falling into comfortable places. My prayer, which I so faithfully recited before each writing session simply went, "God, I want to be a writer, but let's don't do anything drastic about it just now." I reveled in the newfound experience, sensing writing's heady joy but stiff-arming its companion sense of urgency. Time was no problem. Tomorrow seemed, when I took time to think about it, years away. Things were still going up.

Then, at some unnoticed moment, I began to hear that ticking clock inside my head. Probably it was activated by the undeniable growth of my children, particularly Kathi. Their growth forced me, as such growth has forced a billion fathers before me, to recognize my fleeting mortality.

But my writing was also beginning to make mid-life demands, as if possessing a will of its own. What had I proved in nine years of writing? Without anyone to read my work could I be sure that I had improved at all, or that I was any good in the first place? What if I was destined to be nothing more than a prolific pipe dreamer, burning away the evening hours of my life scratching out tedious trivia on stacks of legal pads, which would remain unnoticed until embarrassed and guilt-ridden family members found them and shrugged, wondering what to do with them now that Grandpa was gone?

Thus my leisurely prayer began to take on a note or urgency around 1987. "Now!" I cried, like a jockey in the home turn. "Let's do it now!"

Two visions particularly haunted me. One was of my own Grandpa Knowles, faithfully sending five and ten dollar "investments" to some oil outfit in Texas which was forever assuring him they were on the verge of a big strike. How oddly unlike Grandpa to do such a thing. Intelligent, conservative, disciplined, morally straight almost to the point of Puritanism, Grandpa hardly seemed a candidate for this kind of scam. Apparently there was something irresistible in the hope itself.

And I began to wonder. Was I caught up in the same kind of foolish hope? Was my writing simply my own version of Grandpa's oil wells?

The second vision was more frightening. It was of a nameless old man I recognized all too readily, sitting in a quiet corner somewhere, bitterly wondering why he had never quite gotten around to doing the thing in life he had so clearly been called to do. He had a decent supply of excuses and rationalizations—he was sufficiently smart to concoct enough of these to win sympathetic nods from his friends—but he could never gain lasting comfort from them. He had missed his best chance; now he was doomed to the twilight torture of wondering why.

The exhilaration of divine certainty about my Possibility eventually gave way to confusion, then to anger, the venomous anger of childish self-pity, the kind of thing I thought I had left behind half a lifetime ago. The anger would catch me during idle moments. What would start out cheerily enough as a long bus ride home at the end of a fairly productive day would end in the depths of agitated self-pity. I could physically feel its poison seeping down inside of me, but this carefully nurtured and suppressed anger, which has been medically recognized as a contributor to depression, was too delicious to resist.[64]

Besides, I had little desire to resist it. Where had God gone during the magical moment? Why had God deserted me just when I had finally agreed to go after my Possibility? Most infuriating of all, why had God bothered to infect me with this passion, this calling, if it wasn't going to lead me anywhere?

I thought about the Japanese at Rabaul in New Guinea during World War II. They had placed a magnificent army there, filled with veteran soldiers anxious to die for the emperor. It was still early in the war and they knew there was no way McArthur could beat them. Their problem was that McArthur knew it too. He simply bypassed them, skipping ahead across the Pacific on his historic path, which would eventually take him back to the Philippines and Japan itself. This was the only possibility that the Japanese at Rabaul had not anticipated, and the only one they could not endure. They were left unused. All their preparation and devotion were now turned against them in the form of negative energy. Their spirits crumbled. The magnificent army died without a fight.

I felt that way—unused. Ready for the moment, then bypassed. It stirred a bitterness which surprised me, but I moved over and made room for it. At least there was some company there.

☾

At some time during the early part of 1989 I changed my prayer for the last time. Not unlike Catherine Marshall, I found this final phase of my spiritual metamorphosis wholly lacking in inspiration. The third prayer was less the triumphant find at the end of a faithful soul's journey than the realization that this was the only place I had left to go.

In *The Jungle*, Upton Sinclair's novel about the labor injustices in early twentieth-century Chicago, Sinclair told of the Lithuanian immigrant, Jurgis. With his family facing eviction and starvation, Jurgis got up one morning and decided to go to work in the fertilizer plant. Sinclair described the plant as the place men go when they have reached the bottom of the work world, a place where the putrid stench and diseased coloring of the plant's product soaked deep into the worker's skin and lungs, making him virtually unfit to live with. This was a destination the workers found only when they had despaired of any other kind of job, when everything else had failed.

It was in something like the spiritual equivalent of that condition that I offered this pathetic prayer to God. "All right, if you can't or won't change the circumstances of my life to make me a writer, then I guess there's only one thing left to change: me. If it's absolutely necessary, go ahead."

Deep within I knew such change was essential. My elevated intensity regarding publication had not, during the previous few years, been matched by a similar increase in my writing prolificacy or proficiency. In fact, I was completely bogged down. I had written only one piece of any merit during that period, a couple of short articles for our church newsletter, and these I never intended to publish.

I was a weary traveler, struggling feebly to ascend a mountain of soft sand, but always sliding back to my starting point. The writing fire within me, God's persistent messenger, was not extinguished, but it had been reduced to a still small candle flame uninspired by any wind or movement. I began to think a great deal about that bitter old man spending his long, retirement years in a search of places to lay the blame for missing out on his life's great might-have-been.

My prayer was pounded out of me by this and another, darker, vision. In it I saw the same old man tormented not only by the loss of his Possibility but also by the loss of his faith. Oh, this was no headlong flight to a rationalized atheism, from whence he could laugh at weaker men who needed the fools' gold of religion, nor was it the perpetual option of "curse God and die" such as tempted Job. Nothing quite that easy or clean. He was still attending church and managing to say the right things most of the time, but this was for the benefit of those around him.

Long ago, in my vision, the bitter old man I would become had yielded to the sinister suspicion that this God-thing really doesn't work, that the timeless, godless forces of the world always seem to have their way in the end. He had shut down the deeper recesses of his soul, having consciously decided to avoid the unpleasantries of those regions by staying busy. During those rare moments when nasty questions did force themselves to the surface he would cover everything with a bit of philosophical banality to the effect that "life is just that way," and "that's the way the Man Upstairs operates, I guess." It wasn't so much that he had lost his faith as that he had never quite found it. Now he was too old and tired to try.

And so, with little better incentive than that provided Scrooge by his third apparition, I prayed my third prayer. It was the most difficult of prayers. No one likes to assume personal blame for a failure, especially one into which they have poured great effort and sincerity. And most people would greatly prefer that God meet the needs in their lives by changing physical circumstances, or opportunities, or even other people, rather than themselves. Worst of all, making a request of God can be a dangerous thing. If I had known then how dangerous, I almost certainly would have let not-very-well-enough alone.

The third "P" in my spiritual struggle with problems, paradoxes and possibilities seemed to be sending me in reverse, like Hannah Hurnard's Much Afraid, who often wondered despairingly why the road to the promised high places so often turned down into valleys. I was stunned by the unfathomable sequence of events which followed my prayer. Someone had a weird sense of direction. I had prayed to God about my writing

out of fatigue, anxiety, and despair, with at least some willingness to let go of my compulsive desire to plan and control everything.

What I got in response was a thermonuclear blast of depression which redefined the meaning of the word "fatigue" for me. I
had difficulty eating, lost fifteen needed pounds, and could barely manage daily tasks, much less write books. Was this the stuff
of success?

But I was too far gone to spend much time fretting about injustices and nonsense. A year earlier I would have stood eye to
eye with God, like the self-proclaimed prince, Job, and demand-
ed an explanation. Now I was just concerned with simple survival, thrashing about for any log which might keep me afloat
awhile longer. Life had become menacingly simple.

Simple. That was it. I had been reduced to the original lump
of clay, a smoldering little pile of something which, for whatever
reason, had not burned up with the rest. I had fancied myself in
the final leg of the championship run, crying out to God, like billions of others before me, to just give me a little break. I just
craved that slight edge, that first publication, which would get
me going. Was that asking too much? I would do all the rest.

But I never got the break, nor even the slightest hint of a tail
breeze. And when I, with what I thought was genuine humility,
decided to see if yielding a chunk of my will would gain the result, I suddenly found that I was not only losing the race, I was
not even in it anymore. I was back at the first day of practice,
with constant aches and pains, and goals which seemed impossi-
bly distant. All that was left was this little box with a tiny candle
burning inside.

Then, precisely because of its ridiculous simplicity, the thing
began to make sense. I began to see a cohesion, a oneness, which
both startled and intrigued me. It began where my Faith and
Medical Roles joined in front of my eyes and became one.

In analyzing how I had come to experience such a caldron of
depression I was pleasantly stunned to find that doctors and
Scriptures were telling me the same thing. Anger, bitterness,
self-pity, and impatience reap both medical and spiritual har-
vests of pain because the same rules apply to both.

David the psalmist, pleading with God to lift the depression crushing his spirit, could not have known about the delicately balanced flow of serotonin and norepinephrine in his body. But such knowledge would not have changed the issue for him. David was in emotional trouble, not unlike that which had plagued Saul before him, because he had invited guilt and anger into his life. Anger is a poison, a physical poison, with predictable results. It took us a few thousand years to prove that point medically, and to invent medicines to address it, but the best medicine is still precluding the anger.

Furthermore, I could see that my emotional crisis had not been dropped on me by a God who was clicking his tongue and saying, "Aha! I tried to warn you, but you wouldn't listen," nor a God who was sadly shaking his head in fatherly love and saying, "This is going to hurt me more than it is you." The crisis was not even imposed on me by a God who was saying, "You need this pain as a form of my discipline."

In fact, the crisis was not "dropped" on me at all. It was delivered to me as a very logical consequence of some behavioral choices I made over a period of several years, and in accordance with universal precepts established eons ago by the God of all three quotations. I, unlike others who may suffer depression for reasons over which they have no control, might have avoided my seven months at hell's earthly gate had I chosen not to cross those precepts.

But once in the abyss, what then? Was I forever doomed by my mistake? Now it gets interesting! If the Medical Role and the Spiritual Role were really one, actually different ways of proceeding to the same truth, then might not my Writing Role also be part of that oneness? If God could use pain, even what seemed the excessively cruel pain of emotional upheaval, to reveal answers to the problem and paradox of my faith, might the same pain reveal something to me about my Possibility?

I began to consider the stunning prospect that God's answer to my prayer was going to be fashioned out of the substance of what I thought to be the problem. I began to wonder if the worst anxiety and depression I had ever suffered, and which had been triggered in large measure by my writing frustrations, was going to provide me with the material I needed to reawaken the gift of writing.

(

God used the agony of depression and anxiety to help ease the sickness which had led to the depression and anxiety. How it happened is beyond me, but that it happened is beyond question. The arduous journey to my Possibility began and ended in the same place.

There is a sameness about the advice given by great writers to novice writers. Shorn of other trappings the advice says, "Write what you know and care about." My seven months in the dark hole of anxiety and depression gave me both. I learned about feelings, how people handle them, and what they mean medically, socially, and spiritually.

I found myself devouring a dozen books on the subject within a few months—I, who used to strictly avoid "how-to" books. My appetite was insatiable for this subject which had once held only passing interest for me. Psychiatrists, psychologists, ministers, medical doctors, newspaper reporters, and friends were, it suddenly seemed to me, all obsessed with this one crucial subject. And they were all saying the same things, though dressing the words in the fashions of their personal disciplines or interests.

Here was something important. Here was something that touched me deeply, something I knew about. Here was something I could write about. My three years in the backwashes of the Muse were over. My run for the world's record in writer's block ended in delicious defeat.

Any writer will tell you that wishes, hopes, or prayers do not automatically translate into publications. Publication follows its own weird logic, as any trip to the drugstore bookrack will attest. I don't think God wastes many of those rare interventions Lewis describes on book publications. But in my case, I got the feeling God couldn't resist a subtle foray into the publishing world, nothing more than a footnote to the events of my past year but one of those details small to others yet gigantic to me.

Again the event was tied to that extraordinarily difficult business trip to Key West in September of 1989. A few months earlier, at the suggestion of my minister and an elder in our church, I had submitted for publication several articles about worship which I had written for our church newsletter. As I said before, I had no publishing intentions, other than the newsletter, for the short pieces. I probably had lower expectations for and less concern about this submission than almost anything else I had ever sent to a publisher. The style and format were wrong—church newsletters and national Christian magazines share little in common editorially. How could I get excited about this prospect after sending out dozens of book query letters?

When I arrived home, after Janet, after Hugo, and after my first-ever successful experience in obedience to a divine command, the unopened letter from the publisher was waiting. I didn't see it until an hour or two after I arrived. Lezlee had just stacked it with the other mail from the week; she told me later that she was mad that part of my welcome home had to include another rejection from a publisher.

As I opened the letter, I thought I wouldn't let this spoil what had been a remarkable week. My experienced eye caught the publisher's paid postage on the envelope, but I assigned this no special significance. I assumed they had lost the self-addressed stamped envelope I routinely sent, and which is the only sign most writers have that a publisher ever received their submission.

The letter did not make sense. First, it had been written by a human, not a computer. Second, it offered an opinion on the merit of the work—someone had actually read and liked it. (My eyes were searching vainly for the old, familiar "does not suit our present publishing goals" line which blankets the mounds of good and bad unsolicited materials received by publishers.) Last, the silly people were talking about money and a publication date.

Perhaps only a frustrated writer can fully appreciate the importance of this unique correspondence, but many people can identify with the feelings which arise within when the first installment on a lifelong dream is paid. Even after seemingly endless and fruitless years of working toward the dream, there is the sudden feeling that it cannot be this easy, this quick; something must be wrong.

I could not help grinning at the letter as Lezlee read it over my shoulder. After twelve years of more-or-less continuous devotion to writing, four years in the doldrums of the writer's craft, several months in the icy grasp of emotional upheaval, and seven of the toughest days of my life, I was standing there feeling euphoric. All because of a sixty dollar magazine sale which promised publication, sometime during the next six to eighteen months, of one of the few things I had ever written without any thought of publication.

The event was so far removed from fantasies I had entertained about my "successful" writing career that an embarrassed grin was the only appropriate response. A year earlier I would have seen the event as a cruel joke. Now, having bloodied my entire being in the process of learning the first rudimentary lessons on problems, paradoxes, and possibilities, I could only thank God for this exquisite touch and wonder what other tiny fortunes he might be arranging for me.

Epilogue

It is MID-SEPTEMBER, 1990, nearly fourteen months after my seemingly stable world started coming apart in an Austin, Texas, hotel room. In the wake of a line of thundershowers the sultry summer cycle has been broken. We are left with the first cool hint of things to come. Normally this is the prelude to my favorite time of year. But this year the reminders are too strong.

For the first time in several months I feel some of the dreaded feelings stir. For two days I revisit the valley I walked for an eternity last year. The feeling is instantly recognizable yet, as always, carries with it the terrible capacity to seem wholly new and uniquely threatening. The beast is saying, "I'm back again. Did you really think I would let you go for good? But wait until you see what I have for you this time! This time you won't get away."

The war between my rational and irrational beings resumes in full fury. A calm voice within tells me that all of this is understandable, that depression frequently reoccurs for short periods, that I have actually done well with a very emotional late summer, that my self-imposed reduction in the anti-depressant medication was bound to leave some gaps, that a change in seasons can be an emotional catalyst even without powerfully painful memories such as those I stitched into the fabric of last September.

Another voice, shrill and intimidating, fires off a staccato of what-ifs. What if the prior months, the "good" months, was only a temporary reprieve? What if the medication is no longer effective? What if the rest of my life is doomed to a hopelessly undulating cycle of good springs and summers, followed by disastrous falls and winters? What if my seeming "progress" in recent months has really been just so much self-delusion?

Within a twenty-four-hour period I am struck by the timely relevance of two interviews aired on National Public Radio, both of which seem aimed directly at me. The first, with Kitty Dukakis, reveals that the 1988 would-be First Lady had to interrupt the writing of her recently published book several times during her up-and-down battle with substance abuse. No one wants to read a story about a Herculean struggle against alcoholism if the protagonist ends up losing the battle. The interviewer noted that Dukakis herself was apparently still unsure of the final outcome since she concluded her book with the comment that this was her story—at least to the extent that she knew it.

The second interview, conducted by the same reporter, was with author William Styron. It concerned his cataclysmic struggle with depression in the mid 1980s. With the knowledge of Kitty Dukakis' many relapses fresh on her mind, the interviewer bluntly asked Styron how he could so confidently write about a monster which had nearly killed him only five years earlier. Wasn't he afraid, she probed, that the thing could and would return?

The question haunted me. If it could be asked of Styron five years after his ordeal, how much more relevant was it for me, who dared to write a book about earthquakes while the ground beneath my feet still trembled? Would I, like Dukakis, have to leave my work open-ended, amenable at any moment to a qualifying footnote which would compromise every hard-won answer I had committed to these pages?

My depression's return engagement played only two days, then closed abruptly, as if sensing it did not have much of an audience in this town. But the pain had scored deeply enough to remind me that those answers had been forged in fire, not fat. The fact that they were still too hot to touch told me only *when* they had been crafted for my use. Why, or how, or *that* they had been given to me was beyond dispute.

Everything in life and Scripture cries out to us that we, in this life, are ever in a state of becoming, never in a state of being. A book like this is a milepost, not a destination. Just as the truth about alcoholism is not dependent on what Kitty Dukakis may do tomorrow, neither is the truth about emotional pain dependent on the valleys of depression and anxiety which may yet lie before me. Yet the two of us, she on her road and I on mine, have unique opportunities to serve as mapmakers for others who may come this way. And those maps will remain true regardless of our tendencies to wander off the road in times to come.

But the ultimate justification for daring to write this kind of book is the certainty not that I have forever won the battle with emotional difficulties, but that this battle is fought out on the plain of *real life.* These words address, however feebly, issues at the heart of life's meaning, questions which were important 5,000 ago and will remain important 5,000 years from now. Herein are the elements of real pain, real fear, real joy, and real faith. It is the world of God's original creation—stupendous, awesome, terrifying, electrifying, and always real.

It is the world we have largely lost or rather, abandoned. We have withdrawn from its blinding lights and sandpaper walls to create our own world of reality, a well-insulated nook formed by predigested news, power lunches, and packaged sex. We run it to the clocks of sitcoms, rush-hours, and kickoffs. This is what most people, even Christians, mean by the "real world." It is not a necessarily good world, but neither is it necessarily bad. It is, as the witch contemptuously says in the Broadway play, *Into the Woods,* not good or bad, just nice.[65] In it, even the most religiously oriented people can live for years without being disturbed by the presence of the living—the real—God.

It is not surprising, then, that the devastating impact of depression or anxiety conveys a sense of "unrealness," leaving us stunned, as in the aftermath of a shocking event or in the midst of a nightmare. Real pain is so adamantly excluded from our idea of the real world that we automatically assume it must be, in fact, unreal. Peter may have alluded to this twisted sense of reality when he told the early Christians to "not be surprised at the painful trial you are suffering, as though something strange were happening to you" (1 Pet. 4:12).

This strange, decidedly uncomfortable world is the world of our God, the real world. Almost as soon as I reentered it for those two days in September, I was struck by its rich, bittersweet taste—a taste of struggling, meaning, risking, and growing. And just as before, God was all over me in a second, fairly smothering me with caresses, encouragement, ideas—and a few delicious resting places—little of which he can get to me when I am lingering lethargically on the other side of reality in what we call the real world. The pain cleared my head so I could see what most of us spend a lifetime trying not to see: real meaning, real importance, real life.

I did not stay there long, only those two days. Like the Old Testament patriarchs, who could not stand too much of God's direct presence, I needed to retreat to my nice, plastic world to rest for a while. I think God knows that, save for an exceptional few among us, we cannot tolerate too much pain, even cleansing pain.

But along with me I took a renewed sense of joy as well as the conviction to conclude and let go of my small testimony to God's real world—this book. If nothing else, perhaps it will be a reminder to me, or, perhaps you, that behind everything we see and do in life stands a world of real and eternal truth.

Our task is to reach for it.

Notes

1. C. S. Lewis, *The Problem of Pain* (New York: Macmillan Publishing Co., Inc., 1962), 105.

2. See the description of anxiety symptoms in Frank Minirth, Paul Meier, and Don Hawkins, *Worry-Free Living* (Nashville: Thomas Nelson Publisher, 1989), p. 171.

3. J. Raymond DePaulo and Keith Russell Ablow, *How to Cope with Depression* (New York: McGraw Hill Publishing Company, 1989), 38, 56.

4. Edmund Vance Cooke, "How Did You Die?" *One Hundred and One Famous Poems* (Chicago: R. J. Cook, 1926), 44.

5. Demitri F. Papolos and Janice Papolos, *Overcoming Depression* (Harper & Row, Publishers, 1987), 4.

6. Hannah Hurnard, *Hinds' Feet on High Places* (Wheaton, Ill.: Tyndale House Publishers, Inc., 1975).

7. Minirth, Meier, and Hawkins, *Worry Free Living,* 16.

8. C. S. Lewis, *The Screwtape Letters* (New York: Macmillan Publishing Co., Inc., 1961) 141-142.

9. Lewis, *The Screwtape Letters,* 39.

10. Joe Bob Briggs, "Pop a Prozac and Woes Will End—Or Will They?" *Columbus Dispatch,* March 27, 1990, 11A.

11. Ibid.

12. Enid and Richard Peschel, "Bias Against Mentally Ill Continues," *Columbus Dispatch,* March 12, 1990, 11A.

13. Lewis, *The Screwtape Letters,* 89.

14. Minirth, Meier, and Hawkins, *Worry-Free Living,* 127.

15. Lewis, *The Problem of Pain,* 115.

16. Minirth, Meier, and Hawkins, *Worry-Free Living,* 22.

17. James Dobson, *What Wives Wish Their Husbands Knew About Women* (Wheaton, Ill.: Tyndale House Publishers, Inc., 1975), 143-146.

18. Michael D. Yapko, *When Living Hurts* (New York: Brunner/Mazel, Publishers, 1988), 9.

19. William Wordsworth, "The Happy Warrior," *One Hundred and One Famous Poems,* 27.

20. Tim Hansel, *You Gotta Keep Dancin'* (Anderson, Ind.: The Top in Sound, Inc., 1986), sound cassette.

21. Lewis, *The Problem of Pain,* 156.

22. Minirth, Meier, and Hawkins, *Worry-Free Living,* 46.

23. Lewis, *The Problem of Pain,* 106-107.

24. C. S. Lewis, *The Voyage of the "Dawn Treader"* (New York: Collier Books, Division of Macmillan Co., Inc., 1952), 90.

25. Lewis, *The Problem of Pain,* 156.

26. Kahlil Gibran, *The Prophet* (New York: Alfred A. Knopf, 1968), 52.

27. Hurnard, *Hinds' Feet on High Places,* 66.

28. Darlene Rose, *I Will Never Leave Thee* (Pomona, Calif.: Focus on the Family, 1987), sound cassette.

29. Robert J. Owens, "Wrestling with God," *Springdale* (Birmingham, England: Birmingham College, September 1989).

30. Hansel, *You Gotta Keep Dancin',* sound cassette.

31. Ibid.

32. Lewis, *The Problem of Pain,* 89.

33. Gibran, *The Prophet,* 29.

34. Henry Wadsworth Longfellow, "A Psalm of Life," *One Hundred and One Famous Poems,* 123.

35. Papolos, *Overcoming Depression,* 8.

36. Lewis, *The Screwtape Letters,* 142-143.

37. Philip Yancey, *Disappointment with God* (Grand Rapids, Mich.: Zondervan Books, 1988), 237.

38. Ibid.

39. Lewis, *The Problem of Pain,* 101.

40. Yancey, *Disappointment with God,* 204.

41. Alexander Pope, "An Essay on Man," in *Image and Value,* ed. Martha Heasley Cox (New York: Harcourt, Brace and World, 1966), 499.

42. Don Baker, *Depression: Finding Hope and Meaning in Life's Darkest Shadow* (Portland, Ore.: Multnomah, 1983), 110.

43. C. S. Lewis, *Surprised by Joy* (New York: Harcourt, Brace and Company, 1955), 168.

44. Lewis, *The Screwtape Letters,* 21.

45. Baker, *Depression,* 108-109.

46. Lewis, *The Screwtape Letters,* 28.

47. Papolos, *Overcoming Depression,* 11.

48. I am not suggesting this idea is new or that most counselors once confined themselves to making repairs. But it does seem that today's treatments demand more active patient participation and less of a "fix-it" mentality.

49. Papolos, *Overcoming Depression,* 65-66.

50. Edna St. Vincent Millay, "Renascence," *One Hundred and One Famous Poems* (Chicago: J. R. Cook, 1926), 167-168.

51. Jim Conway, *Men in Midlife Crisis* (Elgin, Ill.: David C. Cook, 1978).

52. Minirth, Meier, and Hawkins, *Worry-Free Living,* 41.

53. Ibid., 28, 114.

54. Lewis, *The Screwtape Letters,* 68, 42.

55. Baker, *Depression,* 55.

56. Lewis, *The Problem of Pain,* 28.

57. Ibid., 19-22.

58. Arthur Hugh Clough, "Say Not, the Struggle Nought Availeth," in *Image and Value,* ed. Martha Heasley Cox, 535.

59. Lewis, *"Dawn Treader,"* 157.

60. Yancey, *Disappointment with God,* 49.

61. Ibid., 59.

62. Lewis, *The Problem with Pain,* 34.

63. Catherine Marshall, *Adventures in Prayer* (Old Tappan, New Jersey: Fleming H. Revell Company, 1975), 52.

64. Yapko, *When Living Hurts,* 11.

65. *Into the Woods* (New York: BMG Music 1988), sound cassette.

The Author

JEFF KNOWLES was born in Cleveland, Ohio, in 1948. His family moved fifteen miles away to Northfield in 1953. Knowles attended Northfield schools through high school.

In 1970 Knowles received a B.A., with a double major in history and philosophy, from Milligan College, a Christian liberal arts college in Tennessee. In 1976 he received an M.A. in history from Georgia State University (Atlanta).

During his Atlanta years (1972-1976), Knowles entered his present field of criminal justice research, via a Georgia State internship under governor Jimmy Carter. This was followed by a tenure with the Georgia State Crime Commission in Atlanta, where he served as a researcher and coordinator of the State Impact Cities program. In 1976 Knowles and his family moved to Columbus, Ohio, where he later became research chief in the Governor's Office of Criminal Justice Services, a post he still holds.

Knowles is married to the former Lezlee Jo Eick, with whom he has raised Kathi (1972) Kimberly (1975), and Mark (1977). The family is actively involved in the Beechwold Church of Christ, with Knowles's involvements including music, Bible school teaching, the eldership, and a variety of leadership roles.